The What And Why Of Church Doctrine

Book One

Water Baptism

Larry Monroe Arrowood

WOODSONG
PUBLISHING

The What And Why Of Church Doctrine

Book One

Water Baptism

Larry Monroe Arrowood

Woodsong Publishing
5989 Spring Meadow Lane
Seymour, IN 47274

www.woodsongpublishing.com
woodsongpublishing@yahoo.com

Cover design by Vision Graphics, Seymour, IN
Printed in the United States of America

ISBN: 978-1-7349323-7-9

The What And Why Of Church Doctrine

Book One

Water Baptism

Larry Monroe Arrowood

WOODSONG
P U B L I S H I N G

The What And Why Of Church Doctrine

Book One

Water Baptism

Larry Monroe Arrowood

Scripture quotations are from THE KING JAMES
VERSION OF THE BIBLE (KJV) unless otherwise noted.

Some Scripture quotations are from THE HOLY BIBLE,
NEW INTERNATIONAL VERSION® NIV® Copyright ©
1973, 1978, 1984 by International Bible Society®
Used by permission. All rights reserved worldwide.

Woodsong Publishing
5989 Spring Meadow Lane
Seymour, IN 47274

www.woodsongpublishing.com
woodsongpublishing@yahoo.com

Cover design by Vision Graphics, Seymour, IN
Printed in the United States of America

ISBN: 978-1-7349323-7-9

Table of Contents

Preface

*And are built upon the foundation of
the apostles and prophets, Jesus Christ
himself being the chief corner stone.*
                              Ephesians 2:20

The Concorde remains but a novelty in history.
The enormous, needle-nose plane, destined to
change aviation from the mundane, now merely
incites questions. Also, regrets. Why did it fail? It
was the joint effort of England and France to lead the
world into a supersonic age. Designed for both high
speed and long distance—necessities in commercial
aviation—it should have outpaced its competitors.
It looked like it would. Here are the stats:

- It took off at 250 miles an hour. The normal
  takeoff speed for jetliners is between 150 and
  180 miles an hour.
- It soared to an altitude of 60,000 feet, almost
  eleven miles high. The typical altitude for
  commercial jetliners is about 36,000 feet.
- It cruised at 1,350 miles per hour, nearly twice

the speed of sound. While the average cruise speed for commercial jetliners is about 500 miles per hour, the Concorde traveled from London to New York in under four hours. A regular commercial flight takes about eight hours.

- When flying west it outraced the sun, so it arrived earlier than it departed.

In October of 2003, the Concorde made its final flight. Instead of being remembered for its speed, it may well be remembered as an example of the folly of pursuing cutting-edge technology at the expense of down-to-earth practicality. My wife, Nancy, and I were in Paris at the Charles de Gaulle Airport in 2000 when the Concorde flight 4590 crashed. We had spent a frustrating drive at the airport, making multiple laps, trying to find the business location to return a rental car. The inconvenience of being unable to read the signs seemed a major issue until, a short time later at our motel, we realized the tragedy that had just happened. All ninety-six passengers and nine flight personnel died, along with some people on the ground. The unheard of for the Concorde had happened, for up to that tragic incident, the Concorde had a perfect flight record.

The Concorde had its advantages, and these seemed to outweigh the drawbacks until this tragedy pushed the weaknesses into the forefront. Here is a list of its problems:

Preface

- It ran into the reality of economics, costing too much for the average customer to pay—$8,000 for a round-trip ticket.
- It could not move the masses, transporting only 100 passengers per trip.
- Because of its speed—breaking the sound barrier and shattering eardrums below—it had few routes it could take over land, so the airport choices were limited.

The one thing it had was speed, but in the end, speed was not enough. It lacked the basics of aviation: economics, moving the masses, and multiple airports that conveniently connected flights. The Concorde had little impact on the masses; coincidentally, the masses make for successful businesses. In contrast, many products cost little but sell to the majority. Typical examples would be fingernail clippers, or a hairbrush, or the cell phone. These cost little, but most need them and can afford to own them; therefore, these are highly favored business products.

Ideas and inventions and programs come and go, but the basics remain virtually the same. Don't get too far from the basics! You may have a great program, but it is incomplete if you try to bypass the basics. Ironically, there is recent talk regarding creating another Concorde-like project. I hope they consider the basics.

But how does the Concorde relate to church

doctrine? Doctrine is the church's basic foundation: what it is built upon. To bypass basics leaves the church vulnerable to failure. A church may be able to build numbers and corral the masses swiftly, but it will never be able to do what God fully desires if it bypasses the fundamental teachings of Scripture.

We can meet the Lord's challenge only if we stick to some basics:

- A consistent prayer time that builds a relationship with Christ,
- A love for and regular study of Scripture,
- Sound doctrine,
- A life that manifests a good Christian witness,
- Faithfulness in attendance and stewardship to a particular Bible-believing church,
- Participation in corporate worship,
- And finally, involvement in some form of church ministry.

Individuals who apply these basics to their lives seldom lose out with God. Even failure is not final; conversely, they have a keen grip on grace, a thorough knowledge of repentance, and a support system to help them return to their first love.

We say, "If only we had some fantastic miracle happen, people would flock to our church." Probably so, but if the basics of salvation are not happening, it is merely a matter of time until everything comes to a grinding halt. Let's share proof from Scripture.

Preface

During some of the greatest miracles, Israel proved faithless. Consider these examples:

- The Egyptian Exodus: The Israelites experienced ten miracles that brought them out of slavery, but a few days later they were murmuring and wishing they were back in Egypt.
- Elijah: Under his ministry, Israel experienced a host of miracles, but as a nation, Israel never recovered from idolatry until after the seventy years of captivity.
- Jesus Christ has no equal in a miracle ministry: Despite all the miracles performed by Christ, in the end, most forsook Him out of disappointment, fear, or ignorance of His more significant purpose in life.

The big challenge is not to seek more miracles; instead, it is a commitment to the basics: daily prayer, consistent study of the Bible, faithfulness to a Bible-believing church, being a positive and consistent witness, bringing people to church with you, getting involved in some form of ministry, and being involved in cooperate worship. These are the foundational stones upon which people of faith build great ministries. The faithful don't follow signs and wonders; rather, signs and wonders follow the faithful. Miracles manifest themselves among the believers. Any ministry that does not follow the basics is building on shifting sand, destined to collapse.

Where does doctrine fit into this picture? Doctrine is the bedrock of the church's foundation. "And are built upon the foundation of the apostles and prophets, Jesus Christ himself being the chief corner stone" (Ephesians 2:20). Doctrine is a culmination of the teachings of both the Old and New Testaments: the prophets of old, the apostles of Christ, and the words of Christ Himself. Further, the apostles were authorized by the Holy Spirit to be the official messengers of the New Testament church:

- They based their message on the teachings of Christ and their knowledge of the Old Testament Scriptures.
- The Holy Spirit assisted in understanding how Christ fit into the message of the Old Testament prophets: "Howbeit when he, the Spirit of truth, is come, he will guide you into all truth: for he shall not speak of himself; but whatsoever he shall hear, that shall he speak: and he will shew you things to come" (John 16:13).
- They proclaimed the message of the New Birth and instructions for believers. We understand their message through a study of the Acts of the Apostles and their instructional writings (epistles) to the first-

century churches.

- We are to follow the teachings of the apostles and continue the mission they started in taking the gospel to the world. I include Paul among the apostles: an explanation comes later in this book.
- A new revelation can never replace the apostles' original revelation: "But though we, or an angel from heaven, preach any other gospel unto you than that which we have preached unto you, let him be accursed" (Galatians 1:18).

I purposefully used few footnotes. The Bible, in various translations, is sufficient to give us all we need to know about God. We can stand before God with confidence if we have followed the Bible. I know of no commentary He has endorsed.

Basics. Nothing fancy. Believing the Word. Daily obeying Christ's commands. Living out the Ten Commandments as were explained by Christ with His landmark Sermon on the Mount. Nothing mystical nor beyond comprehension. Plain enough for a child to comprehend, yet profound enough to allow us the favor of the God Who created the universe.

Part One
Why Doctrine

Take heed unto thyself, and unto the
doctrine; continue in them: for in
doing this thou shalt both save thyself,
and them that hear thee.

I Timothy 4:16

The attack against church doctrine is relentless: some ministers refuse to preach and teach doctrinal issues that are considered controversial. Seminaries challenge the authenticity of the Bible. Church boards usurp pastoral authority and hire and fire depending upon whether or not the pulpit relents to their demands. The laity verbalize what sermons they want to hear and are free to challenge—at will—longstanding doctrines. The government continues to place demands upon the church, which conflict with established tenets of faith. In short, society has tampered with Bible doctrine, watering it down like a diluted medicine: insufficient for spiritual health but favored because of the sweet savor of tolerance.

The Bible is a book of history (the past) and

prophecy (the future). Though old, it is relevant for all time and offers direction for daily living. And it also gives specifics regarding the Christian faith: we call this church doctrine. Let's define what we mean when we speak of biblical doctrine:

> *Bible Doctrine: Beliefs and practices of the church regarding God, salvation, positions on moral and social issues, and principles of lifestyles to which believers should adhere.*

Further, the Bible gives specifics and offers principles for church leaders to teach Apostolic Doctrine (the doctrine taught by the apostles to the first church). I use this term to emphasize the significance of the Apostles in establishing the doctrine of the church. For churches to be genuinely biblical, the leadership must establish and maintain doctrines from Scripture. Some teaching may vary in interpretation from pulpit to pulpit, but for the congregation to remain a Bible-believing assembly, there are core doctrines that leadership should never compromise.

The need for doctrine

From both biblical directives and logic (though human logic should never override Scripture), let's consider the essentiality of Bible doctrine.

Why Doctrine

- God created all things with a distinctive order: you can tell seasons, daily time, and your geographical location by the precise order of the universe. The sky is a clock, a map, and weather reporter.

- Angels (good and evil) must operate from a set of Divine principles. Because Satan rejected God's order of authority, he, along with the angels who followed him, lost their heavenly status. Even though God cast them out of heaven, they must still operate from a set of guidelines ordered by the God of creation. An occasion in the gospels exemplifies where demons expressed their concern that Christ would punish them before the final judgment, because they were subject to Christ's authority (Matthew 8:29).

- For Bible believers who desire to journey in the same direction and to work in harmony to reach a specific destination, Bible doctrine is a uniform guide from which the church can follow.

- In all areas of life, we operate from an established standard. Consider these examples. There are rules (doctrines) that regulate sports. In basketball, how can you tell if you score a point, and how do you know there is a foul? How can you tell when someone scores a touchdown in football?

The answers are simple. Each sport has a set of guidelines. Likewise, there are specific guidelines that regulate the food industry. When you order lunch at a McDonald's restaurant, how can you tell they have not shorted you on fries? They have regular, medium, and large containers. Likewise, guidelines regulate health services: from how to dispense medicine, to the type of clothes the workers must wear. How do we distinguish between the nurses and guests in a hospital? How do we differentiate between custodians and physicians? A list of guidelines determine such. How does the company you work for know what to pay you at the end of the week? They have a course of action to determine whether or not you are doing your work, and these guidelines determine whether or not you get paid and how much you get paid. It is apparent that we need daily guidelines for every area of life. In short, we have many rules—doctrines—for daily living.

- Societal rules are not necessarily convenient for our immediate desires; however, without guidelines, life becomes chaotic. Therefore, we realize the need for safety boundaries in public transportation. What would air travel be like if there were no luggage inspections and limitations of what we can take on

Why Doctrine

a plane? Or what about rules regulating air traffic control? Or how about road transportation? Speed limits? Traffic signs? These are rules for travel safety. Should we do away with safety precautions? Should those who dislike the inconveniences be exempt from the rules? Of course not (except when we're in a hurry). We all understand these principles. They may sometimes seem to be necessary nuisances, but we gladly accept them for the sake of safety and order and peace of mind.

Likewise, there is the need for a set standard of rules within the church. Doctrine acts as the safety boundaries in which individuals, families, and church members can live pleasing to God and be most effective for the Kingdom of God. Doctrine offers specifics regarding God and His dealings with humankind. Doctrine is the skeletal structure that holds the church erect and allows it to advance in a meaningful and uniform direction. Further, doctrine offers protection from the adversary. Were it not for certain doctrines, Satan would have the advantage over us, but even he must follow the guidelines of Scripture regarding his dealing with us. Did not Satan have to get permission from God to attack Job, but permission came with certain parameters.

From the call of Abraham some four thousand years ago, the Jewish people have survived as a distinct race because of their religious doctrine. And their primary doctrine remains intact: monotheism. This was the doctrine that separated Abraham from other religions and continued with Israel as a nation in the wilderness when Moses wrote, "Hear, O Israel: The LORD our God is one LORD: And thou shalt love the LORD thy God with all thine heart, and with all thy soul, and with all thy might" (Deuteronomy 6:4-5). Further, God commanded the Israelites to perpetuate this doctrine. "And these words, which I command thee this day, shall be in thine heart: And thou shalt teach them diligently unto thy children, and shalt talk of them when thou sittest in thine house, and when thou walkest by the way, and when thou liest down, and when thou risest up" (Deuteronomy 6:6-7).

It is the doctrine of monotheism that creates purpose and is a driving and distinctive force within the Jewish community. If we take away the doctrine of monotheism and the teachings associated with this doctrine, the Jewish people cease to be distinctive. They lose their purpose for God's calling. The same is true regarding Christianity. Many Christian churches have lost distinction and purpose because they have abandoned doctrine. Jesus established order and purpose for the church by selecting twelve apostles whom He taught and gave authority to establish the church. "And I say also unto thee, That thou art Peter, and upon this rock I will build my church; and the gates of hell shall not prevail

Why Doctrine

against it" (Matthew 16:18).

Christ's final words to His disciples reinforced the significance of following the teaching of the Old Testament regarding Who He is. Further, He brought clarity to them regarding the Old Testament prophecy and how they were to perpetuate the message:

> And he said unto them, These are the words which I spake unto you, while I was yet with you, that all things must be fulfilled, which were written in the law of Moses, and in the prophets, and in the psalms, concerning me. Then opened he their understanding, that they might understand the scriptures, And said unto them, Thus it is written, and thus it behooved Christ to suffer, and to rise from the dead the third day: And that repentance and remission of sins should be preached in his name among all nations, beginning at Jerusalem. And ye are witnesses of these things. And, behold, I send the promise of my Father upon you: but tarry ye in the city of Jerusalem, until ye be endued with power from on high.
>
> Luke 24:44-49

Consider the authority given the apostles.

Jesus pronounced, "And I will give unto thee the keys of the kingdom of heaven: and whatsoever thou shalt bind on earth shall be bound in heaven: and whatsoever thou shalt loose on earth shall be loosed in heaven" (Matthew 16:19). Further, Christ proclaimed, "Whose soever sins ye remit, they are remitted unto them; and whose soever sins ye retain, they are retained" (John 20:23).

These were the Lord's directives to the apostles before His ascension. All four of the gospel writers affirm the same: the authority and necessity of establishing church doctrine. After the Lord's ascension, and the empowerment of the Holy Spirit, we readily see Christ's commands being fulfilled as the people followed the apostles' doctrine. "Then they that gladly received his word were baptized: and the same day there were added unto them about three thousand souls. And they continued stedfastly in the apostles' doctrine and fellowship, and in breaking of bread, and in prayers" (Acts 2:41-42).

The Apostle Paul, chosen of the Lord specifically to take the gospel to the gentile nations, wrote most of the New Testament. He offered directives to his associates in establishing the church. One of his primary concerns was that the church might abandon established doctrines. Consider his concerns written at length to a young associate, Timothy (I Tim 4:1-16; II Tim 3-4:1-5). His concern can be summed up in one verse among these Scriptures: "Take heed unto thyself, and unto the doctrine; continue in them: for in doing this thou shalt both save thyself, and them that hear thee" (I Timothy 4:16).

Paul also verbalized his concern to the Ephesian church elders. An accompanying minister, Luke the Physician, recorded Paul's concerns:

> Take heed therefore unto yourselves, and to all the flock, over the which the Holy Ghost hath made you overseers, to feed the church of God, which he hath purchased with his own blood. For I know this, that after my departing shall grievous wolves enter in among you, not sparing the flock. Also of your own selves shall men arise, speaking perverse things, to draw away disciples after them.
>
> Acts 20:28-30

The New Testament book of The Acts of the Apostles (some prefer to call this book the acts of the Holy Spirit through the apostles) and the epistles (twenty-one letters written to the first-century churches by known and approved ministers of the gospel) established specific doctrines for the first-century church. These doctrines developed from three primary sources: the moral principles of the Old Testament; the teachings of our Lord to the disciples (recorded in the four gospels); and the divine inspiration of the Holy Spirit—the promised indwelling presence of the Lord that would lead and guide them into all truth: John 16:13— ministering through the apostles. These established doctrines were not mere opinions of the authors, nor were they subject to change by subsequent generations. These were established for all the churches and for all succeeding generations to adhere.

Paul's letters to New Testament churches and ministers expressed the significance of doctrine. In his letter to Timothy, he expressed: "Meditate upon these things; give thyself wholly to them; that thy profiting may appear to all" (I Timothy 4:15). Paul continued this theme in his second letter to Timothy:

> Preach the word; be instant in season, out of season; reprove, rebuke, exhort with all long suffering and doctrine. For the time will come when they will not endure sound doctrine; but after their own lusts shall they heap to themselves teachers, having itching ears; And they shall turn away their ears from the truth, and shall be turned unto fables.
>
> II Timothy 4:2-4

Here are some of the doctrines established by the first-century authors of Scripture that churches today should study, comprehend, and apply.

• Doctrine regarding water baptism

Why Doctrine

- Doctrine regarding the Holy Spirit baptism
- Doctrine regarding God's attributes
- Doctrine regarding sin
- Doctrine regarding holiness
- Doctrine regarding Christ's second coming
- Doctrine regarding eternal punishment
- Doctrine regarding giving
- Doctrine regarding church attendance
- Doctrine regarding communion
- Doctrine regarding the Sabbath
- Doctrine regarding monotheism

The list is long. I've chosen to cover some of these in a series of books: each book representing a particular doctrine. I reiterate that the doctrines of the church were not mere opinions of the Bible writers. As in the Old Testament, New Testament writers were anointed of God. "For the prophecy came not in old time by the will of man: but holy men of God spake as they were moved by the Holy Ghost" (II Peter 1:21). The doctrines expressed in the New Testament are the infallible Word of God drawn from the Old Testament, affirmed and clarified by Christ, confirmed by the Holy Spirit, and established by the Apostles of Christ. Paul, however, warned of the danger of adding to or taking away from Scripture when he wrote:

> But though we, or an angel from
> heaven, preach any other gospel unto

you than that which we have preached
unto you, let him be accursed. As we
said before, so say I now again, if any
man preach any other gospel unto you
than that ye have received, let him be
accursed.

Galatians 1:8-9

As a child, I lived in the Appalachian Mountains
of Eastern Kentucky. Our community was not
easily accessible, for it lacked a roadway, though a
passenger train stopped mornings and evenings. In
the early nineteen-fifties, workers built a graveled
road that connected our isolated community to the
outside world via automobile. However, the workers
constructed the road on the opposite side of the
North Fork of the Kentucky River of our railway
community. Since the budget didn't allow for a
bridge over the river to our small neighborhood, we
were still cut off from normal transportation.

Eventually, even the passenger train ceased
stopping at our community. To give us access to
the new road, the local men constructed a swinging
bridge across the river. When someone coined the
term "swinging bridge" for this crudely constructed
contraption, they certainly knew what they were
talking about. On windy days, or when several
people walked across at the same time (or the time
I rode my bicycle across), it could be frightening—
not to mention dangerous—as it "swung" back and

forth, suspended by two parallel cables across the water. In the interest of safety, workers installed a four-foot-tall wire fence on either side of the rough, plank flooring. This safety feature removed our apprehension of falling off the side of the bridge. With the fencing, parents were comfortable with small children running ahead of them across the bridge. Why? The fence protected from the danger of plunging off the bridge into the water forty feet below. None of us viewed the fence as a barrier to control or manipulate or punish; conversely, the fence served as our friend. Likewise, doctrine is our friend. We shouldn't view doctrine as being mean-spirited and divisive, but it is for our protection. It is God's means of keeping us on the right path and preventing our wandering off (or plunging off) into false teachings. Further, doctrine is Christ's means of directing His bride to meet His expectations.

A concern for the modern church? We want apostolic authority and apostolic results but not apostolic doctrine. But these are a joint deal, a combined package. You can't have one without the other. A watered-down version of God's plan has always been repulsive unto Him. "Hot or cold," Jesus said to the Laodicean church! Anything in between is lukewarm and unacceptable. From the Scripture, we know how Christ feels about that (Revelation 3:15-16). Vomit!

The consideration of this book is the doctrine of Christian baptism. The New Testament established such as a means of becoming a part of the family of Christ. Not only did Jesus establish the doctrine of baptism through example and oral instruction, He commanded the apostles to teach and practice this doctrine.

> Go ye therefore, and teach all nations, baptizing them in the name of the Father, and of the Son, and of the Holy Ghost: Teaching them to observe all things whatsoever I have commanded you: and, lo, I am with you always, even unto the end of the world. Amen.
> Matthew 28:19-20

> And he said unto them, Go ye into all the world, and preach the gospel to every creature. He that believeth and is baptized shall be saved; but he that believeth not shall be damned.
> Mark 16:15-16

The Apostles never wavered regarding water baptism for converts. With such direct commands from Christ, and with the multiple examples of baptisms in Scripture, we dare not overlook the significance of baptism.

Part Two
Christ And The Apostles' Role In Establishing Doctrine

Jesus saith unto him, I am the way, the truth, and the life: no man cometh unto the Father, but by me.

John 14:6

The Pharisees dropped their guard when Christ proclaimed, "Think not that I am come to destroy the law, or the prophets: I am not come to destroy, but to fulfil" (Matthew 5:17). That must have consoled their self-righteous hearts, for they doggedly clung to their convoluted teachings by distorting the Old Testament Scripture. And they managed the masses by their interpretation of the Mosaic Law. They could quote a verse for every deed, every tradition, and every religious act they committed. Perhaps this young whippersnapper from nowhere of significance was okay after all.

To their utter disappointment, Christ followed that statement with one to which they recoiled in shock. "For I say unto you, That except your righteousness shall exceed the righteousness of the scribes and Pharisees, ye shall in no case enter into the kingdom of heaven" (Matthew 5:20). Thus began a new era of doctrine, an elevated bar of expectation, and Christ's new doctrine cut to the heart, for it bypassed the scrutiny of man's intellect and focused upon the intent of God. Jesus affirmed that you should carry the adversary's burden the necessary mile that the common rule required, but He further admonished, as a gage to determine if the heart was clean of bitterness, go an extra mile (Matthew 5:41). Jesus challenged them as being skin-deep performers, and He compared them to the "whited sepulchers" dotting the hillsides, looking rather picturesque externally "but full of dead men's bones" (Matthew 23:27).

Jesus did not come to change the law; He came to redirect men back to the heart of the lawgiver: justice and truth enveloped in mercy. His doctrine differed from the Jewish religious leaders of His day in that His approach, not only raised the bar for righteousness, but He challenged their righteousness as being superfluous. He never added a set of new laws; instead, He went to the core of the problem regarding the laws already on the books. A tranquil brook of truth had evolved into multiple tributaries that ran amuck, making it difficult, if not impossible, for one to find their way. And each of the commands had their commentaries: by which the Pharisees

Christt And The Apostles' Role

controlled the people.

The primary problem with Pharisaism was that it made one's commitment to God primarily external. Their focus was mostly skin deep. They never examined their hearts; rather, they kept a tally of their deeds. They advocated strict observance of external conduct without regard to compassion and forgiveness. In the process, they had become extremely self-righteous, but man's righteousness is never righteous, for at best it is still prideful. So, since the Pharisees falsely professed themselves to be righteous, Jesus called them hypocrites.

For the Pharisees, an act was right or wrong according to some external condition. For instance, there was a difference in giving alms on the Sabbath than on other days. It mattered whether or not the beggar put his hand within the door of the alms giver, or the alms giver stretched his hand beyond his door to place the coin in the beggar's hand. You could curse the beggar in your heart for being poor, or you could begrudge him of the gift that you really didn't want to give him, and that was acceptable, so long as you didn't break the rule of the Sabbath by stretching forth your hand too many inches in your attempt to feed the poor.

A paraphrase of Jesus' teaching could be: "Enough of this nonsense. Let's get back to the heart of giving of alms and the observance of the Sabbath." It's in the heart that evil begins: take care of the heart. Anger and jealousy and revenge and lust and pride, all these and more, germinate and grow in the heart. Nip the problem in the bud, instead of waiting until you have a full-fledged sin issue.

Fifteen hundred years before Christ, Moses had ascended Mount Sinai to receive the Law of God, breaking it in anger before he descended the mountain because he could hear the people below in revelry as they blatantly broke the first and most important of the ten rules. It was apparent the people needed the parameters of the law to guide them. So, following God's instructions, Moses marched back up the mountain to receive another copy. Throughout the years the Mosaic Law had evolved into an accumulation of oral teachings that regulated every waking hour of the Jewish populace. The guidelines originally given to safely steer their lives became bars that held them captive. The Apostle Peter later described the teachings as "... a yoke upon the neck of the disciples, which neither our fathers nor we were able to bear" (Acts 15:10). Jewish teachers had served up the law on cold platters of condemnation and control, but their menu lacked an important ingredient: the Spirit of the lawgiver. By the time Christ appeared on the scene, the religious leaders had distorted the Mosaic Law, and they used their added interpretations to control the masses. So, the original author of the book, the master teacher, ascended a mount in Galilee and expounded the heart of the law. He did not distort nor disavow the Ten Commandments; rather, He elaborated on the

Christ And The Apostles' Role

intent of the commands. Christ's teachings were more a revelation of the nature of God than the commands of God. While the Pharisees stressed, "Do this, and you won't die," Christ stressed, "Do this, and you will live and find happiness in life." Further, Christ challenged the religious leaders' exasperating interpretations of the commands of the Old Covenant: "It hath been said ... But I say unto you ..." (Matthew 5:31-32).

Paul also evaluated the difference between the Old Law of judgment and the New Covenant of grace when he wrote: "Who also hath made us able ministers of the new testament; not of the letter, but of the spirit: for the letter killeth, but the spirit giveth life" (II Corinthians 3:6). He further explained, "Wherefore the law was our schoolmaster to bring us unto Christ, that we might be justified by faith" (Galatians 3:24). The Old Law revealed the sinfulness of humankind and his need for a savior to take care of those sins.

The apostles of Christ acknowledged Him as the missing link in the Old Covenant. It was through the lens of Calvary's grace that they reviewed the Old Law. In so doing, they did not abandon their Jewish faith; they incorporated the needed element of grace, and this new covenant came with an acceptable sacrifice for their sins. The entire Old Testament hinged upon the death, burial, and resurrection of Jesus Christ. These three acts completed—or as Christ said, fulfilled—the Old Testament Law.

And with the added anointing of the indwelling Holy Spirit, the apostles were commissioned of God to interpret the Old Testament, but this time in the light of Christ's atoning sacrifice. In so doing, they established the doctrines of the church, not as a yoke—too heavy to be borne—but as a friend to guide the believer through the treacherous wilderness of life.

Part Three
Paul's Role In Establishing Doctrine

But thou hast fully known my doctrine, manner of life, purpose, faith, longsuffering, charity, patience,

II Timothy 3:10

Though not one of the original twelve apostles, the Lord called Saul of Tarsus (his Jewish name) or Paul (his Roman name) with a unique plan in mind: to take the gospel to the Gentiles. Not only did Paul travel extensively throughout the Roman Empire, establishing churches and church leaders, he wrote several letters of instruction to the churches and to his fellow workers. Paul offered directives to his associates in establishing churches, and he expressed his concern regarding the departure from established doctrine.

Having spent years studying under the famed, Jewish scholar, Gamaliel, Paul was extremely knowledgeable of the Old Testament Law. He understood that some of the teachings of Judaism were a covenant commitment of the nation of Israel to Jehovah and had nothing to do with salvation through Christ. Being Jewish, he observed some of the traditions of the Old Covenant, but he strongly taught that salvation could not be obtained by participation in the Old Testament sacrificial system; rather, salvation came only through Jesus Christ's atoning sacrifice.

Further, Paul interpreted certain Old Testament Laws in light of Christ's sacrifice. In so doing, he challenged as unnecessary for salvation many of the teachings of the Old Testament, primarily the sacrificial system, dietary regulations, and certain social issues. Though he gave liberty for the Jewish Christians to practice the teachings of the Law, so long as they did not claim salvation through the works of the Law, he defended the Gentile church in not obeying all the Jewish covenant rules. However, he stressed certain teachings of the Old Testament that were associated with the morality of God: these never change, and he taught the Gentile church how they should obey these doctrines of God.

Due to Paul's extensive writings to the churches, we are privileged to have these teachings as a part of the doctrine of the church. Ironically, some today try to discredit Paul's writings, suggesting he took too much authority upon himself and that the modern church gives too much attention to his letters. Further, some who claim the Christian faith, but who delve extensively into Judaism, are particularly

Paul's Role

opposed to Paul's teachings, for he challenged the Jewish traditions as unnecessary for salvation: "Let no man therefore judge you in meat, or in drink, or in respect of an holyday, or of the new moon, or of the sabbath days" (Colossians 2:16). This attitude isn't new, for Paul contended with Jewish Christians who imposed Judaic traditions upon fellow believers. (Such traditions were unassociated with God's morality but were ceremonial rituals and traditions associated with the covenant made with Israel. These were mere patterns of Christ and Calvary.

Paul wrote to Timothy expressing concern regarding novices attempting to interpret the extensive and complicated Law of Moses, trying to assimilate the more than six-hundred Jewish regulations into Christianity. He summed up the result of such attempts: "Desiring to be teachers of the law; understanding neither what they say, nor whereof they affirm" (I Timothy 1:7). Due to a host of challenges Paul wrote regarding the erroneous mingling of Judaism and Christianity, some today attempt to discredit his authority, picking and choosing from his writings. Conversely, it is essential that we recognize Paul's God-given authority in writing to the Gentile churches, and it is significant that we accept the doctrines he taught.

When we discredit the authority of Paul, this greatly reduces the New Testament, perhaps by as many as thirteen books, depending on whether we consider Paul the author of The Book of Hebrews. To discredit Paul, and disallow his writings, leaves us with the four gospels, only the first part of The Book of Acts, the two epistles of Peter, The Epistle of James (the brother of our Lord, not the Apostle James), Jude, the three Epistles of John, and The Book of Revelation. Still, if we discredit Paul, some of these books would have to be discredited because they affirmed the ministry of Paul and his teaching.

Consider the domino effect in discrediting the Apostle Paul's authority in establishing doctrine. The greater part of The Book of Acts is eliminated because much of the writings is the record of Paul's missionary endeavors. The gospel of Luke could be discredited because the author, Luke the physician, not only wrote The Book of Acts, which affirms Paul's ministry, but traveled with Paul on much of his missionary journey. The Apostle Peter's two books could be discredited because he also affirmed Paul's writings in one of his own letters to the believers:

> And account that the longsuffering of our Lord is salvation; even as our beloved brother Paul also according to the wisdom given unto him hath written unto you; as also in all his epistles, speaking in them of these things; in which are some things hard to be understood, which they that are

unlearned and unstable wrest, as they
do also the other scriptures, unto their
own destruction.

II Peter 3:15-16

The Book of James could also be in question
because he gave approval for Paul's doctrine at the
first recorded church council in Jerusalem: "… it
seemed good unto us, being assembled with one
accord, to send chosen men unto you with our
beloved Barnabas and Paul, men that have hazarded
their lives for the name of our Lord Jesus Christ"
(Acts 15:25-26).

After eliminating the New Testament books and
authors affirming Paul, we are left with only eight
New Testament books: I, II, and III John, Jude,
Revelation, and the Gospels according to Matthew,
Mark, and John. That's eight of the twenty-seven
books of the New Testament remaining, while
nineteen are in question by discrediting Paul and
those who affirmed his writings.

In discrediting Paul and multiple doctrines
relevant to Christianity, we are left with the gospels
as the dominant writings for Christianity, which
were written relevant to the dispensation of The Old
Testament Law. Sadly, Christians who delve into
Judaism tend to focus upon the Mosaic Law: Jewish
traditions without Calvary's sacrifice. Paul warned
the Galatian church regarding this trap of reverting
from Calvary's sacrifice to the works of the law.

> O foolish Galatians, who hath
> bewitched you, that ye should not
> obey the truth, before whose eyes
> Jesus Christ hath been evidently set
> forth, crucified among you? This only
> would I learn of you, Received ye the
> Spirit by the works of the law, or by
> the hearing of faith? Are ye so foolish?
> having begun in the Spirit, are ye now
> made perfect by the flesh?
>
> Galatians 3:1-3

On the other hand, some within the modern Christian community use Paul as their source of inspiration for throwing off disciplinarian teachings of the church: calling it Christian liberty. In the past seventy-five years, this action has recreated a church unrecognizable by Scripture because it is void of doctrine. These use Paul's letters to the Gentile churches to eliminate certain teachings regarding spiritual disciplines relating to modesty and moderateness, such as: how a Christian should dress, how the believer should behave, what places believers shouldn't frequent, events we shouldn't participate in, and the issue of separation of the sexes. By isolating Scripture, removing it from its intended context, and throwing in a message of grace that excuses sin instead of dealing with it, the modern church allows parishioners to live among, and in harmony with, the lifestyles established by non-

Paul's Role

believers, while feeling no personal condemnation. To discredit Paul's warnings regarding separation from the world by focusing only upon his message of grace, redefines the term "holiness," leaving it up to the whims of the dominant voices. This has come about because some have redefined Paul's statement regarding Christian liberty. Their teaching amplifies grace in such a way as to eliminate any concern for sin. The typical testimony sounds something like, "I'm so glad Jesus died for my sins, so I am now free to keep on sinning without experiencing any guilt or consequences."

Those who disqualify Paul as having apostolic authority, or have misinterpreted his message of grace, are able to embrace a distorted message of cheap grace. Such false teaching of grace justifies one to continue in sin without feeling any guilt, while one picks and chooses regarding certain issues addressed in Scripture. A simple "that's just Paul's opinion" explanation eliminates a host of biblical doctrines embraced by the first church. To willfully or ignorantly profess "I follow Paul's message of spiritual liberty, so I am definitely free to sin without consequences," is to completely distort Paul's message of Christian liberty.

Paul contended with two extreme groups within the church: one, antagonistic Jewish converts to Christianity who clung to the ceremonial customs of Judaism as essential for salvation: circumcision, the temple rituals, and dietary regulations. The second group was Gentile Christians who stretched grace as if it was a rubber band, endless in its flexibility and tolerance of sin. Paul's adversaries attacked him from two angles. He had to contend with the Jewish sect of Pharisees who had become Christians, and who constantly challenged his teachings regarding grace. These contended that salvation came through Christ and strict adherence to the law of circumcision and other Jewish rituals. In contrast to this group, he had the Christian antinomians, whom he challenged regarding their teachings about grace. They contended the more you sin, the greater that makes God's grace as He continues to forgive you. So, sin at will while you testify of God's great grace. This is not to mention the non-Christian, Jewish antagonists who perceived him as an apostate Jew and followed him from city to city, stirring up trouble even to the point of attempting to murder him. Some professing Christians challenged Paul in the first century; some still challenge him still. Yet, why would any Christian attempt to discredit Paul and his writings as authority for the modern church? Probably because his teachings challenge the modern church, holding us to a higher mark than many care to live. And modern Christians who delve into Judaism—intrigued by some of its rituals to the point of setting it alongside Calvary in significance—fall into a category already established by Paul in one of his epistles. "O foolish Galatians, who hath bewitched you ...?" (Galatians 3:1).

Paul's Role

It is important that we consider reasons affirming Paul's writings as being relevant for today's church. First, Paul both affirmed and was affirmed by the teachings of the Apostles regarding the early church doctrine of the new birth and his teaching to the Gentiles regarding grace. Paul made two trips to Jerusalem to confer with the Apostles regarding the message he taught. "Then after three years I went up to Jerusalem to see Peter, and abode with him fifteen days" (Galatians 1:18). He further writes:

> Then fourteen years after I went up again to Jerusalem with Barnabas, and took Titus with me also. And I went up by revelation, and communicated unto them that gospel which I preach among the Gentiles, but privately to them which were of reputation, lest by any means I should run, or had run, in vain. But neither Titus, who was with me, being a Greek, was compelled to be circumcised: And that because of false brethren unawares brought in, who came in privily to spy out our liberty which we have in Christ Jesus, that they might bring us into bondage: To whom we gave place by subjection, no, not for an hour; that the truth of the gospel might continue with you. But of these who seemed to be somewhat,

(whatsoever they were, it maketh no matter to me: God accepteth no man's person:) for they who seemed to be somewhat in conference added nothing to me: But contrariwise, when they saw that the gospel of the uncircumcision was committed unto me, as the gospel of the circumcision was unto Peter; (For he that wrought effectually in Peter to the apostleship of the circumcision, the same was mighty in me toward the Gentiles:) And when James, Cephas, and John, who seemed to be pillars, perceived the grace that was given unto me, they gave to me and Barnabas the right hands of fellowship; that we should go unto the heathen, and they unto the circumcision.

Galatians 2:1-9

Second, Paul's message of grace disputed the Gentile Christians' need to participate in the ceremonial and dietary laws that some within the Jewish Christian community continued to participate. The Jerusalem church leadership, in the first recorded church counsel, established guidelines for the Gentile church, which gave them extreme liberty regarding Jewish rituals (but this did not change the laws regarding morality). This council (specifically Peter and Jesus' brother, James)

Paul's Role

admonished morality among the Gentile believers but gave the Gentile church liberty from the Judaic ceremonial rituals and dietary restrictions. The counsel requested the Gentile converts adhere to the Jewish rituals regulating the eating of blood and to abstain from meats offered to idols. This particular requirement was for the sake of unity among the Gentile and Jewish churches: they were not essential for salvation.

> Then pleased it the apostles and elders with the whole church, to send chosen men of their own company to Antioch with Paul and Barnabas; namely, Judas surnamed Barsabas and Silas, chief men among the brethren: And they wrote letters by them after this manner; The apostles and elders and brethren send greeting unto the brethren which are of the Gentiles in Antioch and Syria and Cilicia. Forasmuch as we have heard, that certain which went out from us have troubled you with words, subverting your souls, saying, Ye must be circumcised, and keep the law: to whom we gave no such commandment: It seemed good unto us, being assembled with one accord, to send chosen men unto you with our beloved Barnabas and Paul, Men that

have hazarded their lives for the name of our Lord Jesus Christ. We have sent therefore Judas and Silas, who shall also tell you the same things by mouth. For it seemed good to the Holy Ghost, and to us, to lay upon you no greater burden than these necessary things; That ye abstain from meats offered to idols, and from blood, and from things strangled, and from fornication: from which if ye keep yourselves, ye shall do well. Fare ye well.

Acts 15:22-29

Note, the restrictions placed upon the Gentile Christians consisted of a couple rituals that were very offensive to some of the Jewish Christians: eating meats sacrificed to idols and observance of food preparation relating to blood. It also demanded they abstain from moral impurity (fornication). Depending on what account you are reading, these three to four demands is a far cry from the over six hundred regulations of the Mosaic Law. This council, however, dealt with ceremonial laws, not moral laws, for God's moral laws never change: they existed prior to the Mosaic Law. So, we know that there were other parts of the Mosaic Law that the Gentile church would have adhered to, specifically the Ten Commandments and laws related to them, not just these three or four mentioned by the council.

Paul's Role

But the long list of traditions, and ceremonial rituals, and observances were excluded.

Third, the decision of the Jerusalem church council did not limit Paul from establishing additional guidelines for godly living among the Gentile believers, it was simply the Jerusalem church leaders' minimum requirements in order for the Gentile believers and the Jewish believers to live harmoniously as brothers in Christ. Conversely, in Paul's writings to the churches, he established certain doctrines regarding how Gentile Christians should live above and beyond these guidelines handed down by the Jerusalem church leaders. This is disconcerting for some churches today, which stress personal liberty regarding one's conscience, disregarding the teachings of Paul regarding specifics for a Christian lifestyle. His emphatic answer to his question to the Romans regarding grace and sin is in conflict with how many modern believers desire to live. "What shall we say then? Shall we continue in sin, that grace may abound? God forbid. How shall we, that are dead to sin, live any longer therein?" (Romans 6:1-2).

Fourth, the doctrine regarding the new birth—as practiced by Paul and is recorded by Luke in the Book of Acts—is in harmony with the message of salvation preached at the birth of the church. To discredit Paul's practice of water and Spirit baptism makes it easier to adopt post apostolic false and incomplete teachings regarding the new birth.

Fifth, Paul addressed multiple issues which are relevant for Christianity today:

- He challenged the Apostle Peter to speak a sound and uniform doctrinal message among Jews and Gentiles regarding fellowship among believers.
- He challenged the tolerance of sin by church leaders.
- He specifically addressed sexual immorality tolerated within the church and demanded it be dealt with by church leaders.
- He addressed the inability of the church to settle disputes among themselves rather than bringing lawsuits among believers into the civil court.
- He attacked carnal thinking about truth.
- He confronted attitudes regarding Christian liberty and clarified the subject of what we are liberated from.
- He wrote directives regarding marriage and divorce.
- He reinforced the teaching of a divine order of authority, including women's role within the body of Christ.
- He encouraged them to develop spiritual gifts in ministry. Further, he gave guidelines for the operation of the spiritual gifts and demanded an orderly demonstration of the same.
- He gave much instruction regarding giving.

Paul's Role

- He challenged the Jewish Christian's belief regarding circumcision being associated with salvation.
- He demanded consistent church attendance by believers.
- He gave commands regarding communion.
- He introduced new teaching regarding the significance of the Sabbath: the spirit of the Sabbath.
- He negated the Jewish law regarding the eating of certain meats.
- He gave instruction for the differentiation of the sexes.

With such numerous teachings addressed by Paul, some feel he took upon himself too much authority and argue his teachings were for local assemblies, addressing local customs of that day. Therefore, some conclude, Paul's teachings are not relevant for the Twenty-first Century church. Conversely, I disagree. To challenge Paul's teachings as relevant for the present church is to challenge the basis for most Christian doctrine. We have fundamentally broken the back of Christianity, rendering it weak and ineffective as a life changing and life directing source. Without doctrine, we are left in a vulnerable state, for in so doing, we have no certain defense against that which is false.

Such was the case in the Old Testament shortly after Israel's settlement in the Promised Land.

Due to the dividing of the land among the tribes of Israel, they spread throughout the land, some of them extremely isolated from the consistent and central leadership. Without direct leadership, they fell into a state where every man began to do that which was right in his own eyes (Judges 21:25). With this attitude, we read accounts among the chosen of God that were abnormal: an individual home having a personal priest. And other accounts were absolutely unthinkable among the Israelites, such as: the practice of idolatry, or a priest slicing his concubine into twelve sections and sending those body parts throughout the tribes of Israel to make a statement against homosexuality and the debauchery that had transpired (Judges 19). God's remedy for that generation? He sent judges. Why? To establish a specific voice from heaven. As it was back then, the lack of specific, Bible doctrines today can be a road to chaos for the Christian movement. That is why doctrine is so very important. Doctrine becomes a clarion voice within the church.

For the sake of including biblical doctrine within the church, it is significant that we include Paul's writings. Here is a list of reasons why we should accept his authority regarding doctrine as the Apostle to the Gentiles:

- He was the most noted teacher of the first church whose teachings survived in written form. If we reject his writings, we are on a

Paul's Role

course of rejecting most of the New Testament. If we reject the New Testament, we have removed the foundation of the church, for all we know about Christ is substantiated by Scripture.

- He was an authority on the Jewish faith, schooled in the Old Testament, and he could speak from personal practice of the Jewish faith, far more advanced than what any modern student of Judaism can understand about First Century Judaism (Acts 22:38; Philippians 3:5-7). Still, some today feel they are more qualified than Paul to interpret Scripture as to how Jesus meant his church to operate. Such an attitude is somewhat comparable to me taking a course in government and then challenging the authority of Thomas Jefferson in writing the Declaration of Independence, as if I know more about what the founding fathers believed than Mr. Jefferson knew.

- He was able to read and understand the oldest Old Testament copies of the Law that were in existence at the time of Christ. He studied at the feet of the grandson of one of the finest Jewish scholars of all time. Paul's in-depth study of Old Testament Scripture, and his personal experience of conversion, along with a three-year study of how the Christian faith harmonized with Old Testament Scripture, qualified him to determine the distinction between the unchanging moral law of God included in the Mosaic Law in contrast to the ceremonial rituals of the temple, dietary regulations, and civil laws (which he termed works or works of the Law) of the five books of Moses. In understanding this distinction, he was able to clarify what parts of the Mosaic Law the Gentile church should obey and what parts they could omit.

- He had a personal unique calling from the Lord—Jesus actually appeared to him. The Apostles at Jerusalem never challenged the personal testimony of Paul's calling; rather, they affirmed him as being the chosen Apostle for the Gentiles.
- He gave up his prestigious position and future in Judaism for the persecuted and self-sacrificing calling as missionary to the Gentile world, ultimately facing martyrdom for the sake of the gospel.
- There is not one scriptural reference of the Apostles ever challenging his doctrine, his calling, his life, or his right as an Apostle to the Gentiles. To the contrary, two influential leaders of the Christian church gave him their approval: both Peter and James.
- Luke, the educated physician, affirms the ministry of Paul. He is the writer of two books in the New Testament. He wrote the Gospel of Luke, which records the Lord's

birth, ministry, death, resurrection, and ascension. He continued his writings with the Book of Acts, which records the descent of the Holy Spirit on the Day of Pentecost. Luke accompanied Paul on some of his missionary journeys, had firsthand knowledge of Paul's ministry, and thus recorded the only historical account of the first church, in which he affirmed both the ministry of the Apostles and the ministry of Paul.

- The Book of Acts (which could rightly be called the Acts of the Holy Spirit), is critical for the establishment of doctrine for the church, and it records Paul's unique and personal call and visitation from the Lord.

It is therefore absolutely right and necessary to include the teachings of the Apostle Paul in our study of doctrine.

Part Four
The Doctrine of Water Baptism

And whatsoever ye do in word or deed,
do all in the name of the Lord Jesus,
giving thanks to God and the Father
by him.

Colossians 3:17

In many church settings, sincerity has supplanted Scripture. In the process, Christian baptism has gone the way of home cooking: it's inconvenient and too traditional. And far too many converts have never experienced the scriptural fact associated with Christian baptism: sins are washed away instead of reasoned away. Many believe that so long as you are sincere, you can chart your own course into heaven. Some further contend the church's insistence that salvation is obtained through obedience to scriptural directives is intolerant, judgmental, and narrow-minded. Regardless of opinions, the Bible regards baptism as essential for the new birth experience.

To reject baptism is to:

- Sidestep direct commands of Scripture,
- Break from biblical examples, and
- Disregard the association of baptism with Christ's death to atone for one's sins.

If we should consider no additional proof, though there is much evidence to support baptism, the fact that Christ submitted to baptism—specifically for our example—screams of baptism's significance. We will, therefore, consider Christ's baptism, and we will explore the multiple examples of Scripture regarding baptism. There are at least four questions that need consideration: Why be baptized? Who should be baptized? When should one be baptized? How should one be baptized?

Why be baptized?

Baptism has its origin in the Old Testament. The Scripture compares the account of Noah and the flood to baptism and thus links baptism with salvation from sin. The Apostle Peter, whom Christ handed the keys that unlock the door into the Kingdom of God, referred to this Old Testament event as being a figure for Christian baptism. "... eight souls were saved by water. The like figure whereunto even baptism doth also now save us ..." (I Peter 3:20-21). Noah did not offer multiple ways to be saved from the flood; conversely, there was only one way—entering into the ark, which was an act of obedience and faith. Sadly, only eight people survived the flood. Why? Was it because God didn't care about His creation? Was it because obtaining salvation had too big a cost? Too risky? No, it was because only eight people entered into the ark, which was God's only means of deliverance.

Contrary to wishful thinking, the Scripture doesn't stretch the numbers regarding redemption; instead, it narrows the odds. Jesus warned, "For many are called, but few are chosen" (Matthew 22:14). "Enter ye in at the strait gate: for wide is the gate, and broad is the way, that leadeth to destruction, and many there be which go in thereat: Because strait is the gate, and narrow is the way, which leadeth unto life, and few there be that find it" (Matthew 7:13-14). God, Who doesn't only love, but Who actually is love, rules the world with a set of determined guidelines regarding redemption. Baptism, in its various typologies, has been a part of redemption since the flood.

God included baptism in the covenant law with Israel. Prior to ministering before the Lord in the Tabernacle, and later in temple worship, the Jewish priests submitted to a ritual cleansing: a type of baptism.

> And the LORD spake unto Moses, saying, Thou shalt also make a laver of brass, and his foot also of brass, to wash withal: and thou shalt put it between

the tabernacle of the congregation
and the altar, and thou shalt put water
therein. For Aaron and his sons shall
wash their hands and their feet thereat:
When they go into the tabernacle of
the congregation, they shall wash with
water, that they die not; or when they
come near to the altar to minister, to
burn offering made by fire unto the
LORD: So they shall wash their hands
and their feet, that they die not: and it
shall be a statute for ever to them, even
to him and to his seed throughout their
generations.

Exodus 30:17-21

Archaeologists have unearthed numerous
baptisteries, which they assert were used in ritual
cleansing by those of the Jewish faith. The monastic
community of Qumran, believed by scholars to be
inhabited by the Essenes from about 135 BC until
around AD 68, practiced ritual bathing, "a symbolic
act of spiritual purification."[1]   Orthodox Jewish
women still participate in monthly ritual cleansing.

More recently, some have argued against
archaeological sites of stepped pools as having been
used for ritual purity practices. However, an article
in BAR unequivocally refutes this claim. Yonatan
Adler writes: "The case for associating stepped
pools ... with Jewish purity concerns couldn't be

The Doctrine Of Water Baptism

more watertight and rock solid."[2]

John the Baptist, the forerunner of Christ, baptized the masses. What an inconvenience for both him and the multitudes who submitted to this spiritual cleansing! Likewise, Christ's disciples baptized converts, and baptism (with its uniqueness) remained a part of New Testament church teaching. In the history of the early church, the ministers baptized all converts: we find no exceptions. Further, all nationalities were included in baptism: Jews, Gentiles, and Samaritans.

Some New Testament writers drew from the account of the Israelites' Exodus from Egypt and compared the manner of deliverance—from their Egyptian bondage—to the deliverance of sinners through Christian baptism. In comparison, the four hundred years of enslavement of God's people in Egypt represents the bondage of sin upon all humanity. In further comparison, Pharaoh and his court magicians were a part of a nature-worshiping religious system. Using the power of evil spirits to work wonders, they tried to keep Israel in bondage by deception. Pharaoh offered Moses a compromise: "Stay in Egypt … we have miracles here too … Egypt is a religious nation ... we have multiple gods, not just one … you don't have to do things Jehovah's way to be saved." But God spoke a succinct message through Moses to those who were in bondage: "Come out of Egypt and separate yourselves unto the one and only true God." How did the Hebrews escape the bondage of Egypt? The Apostle Paul explained the process: "Moreover, brethren, I would not that ye should be ignorant, how that all our fathers were under the cloud, and all passed through the sea; And were all baptized unto Moses in the cloud and in the sea ..." (I Corinthians 10:1-2). On the one side of the Red Sea they were in bondage to sin, and they were subjects of Pharaoh who hated them. Once they went through the sea—symbolic of baptism—they were free from the bondage of sin. Baptism separated them from Pharaoh—who despised them—and Egyptian control; in contrast, they were now subjects to Jehovah, who loved them.

Why be baptized? On this side of baptism, we are in bondage to sin and are subjects of the devil who hates us. Once we experience the waters of baptism, we are freed from our sins and belong to Jesus Christ who loves us. The Apostle Paul instructed his associate, Titus: "Not by works of righteousness which we have done, but according to his mercy he saved us, by the washing of regeneration ..." (Titus 3:5). Bible commentators explain that the phrase "washing of generation" was a reference to Christian baptism. Smith's Dictionary of the Bible states: "All ancient and most modern commentators have interpreted it of baptism."[3]

Why be baptized? The Bible directs baptism by both example and commandment. As noted before, some in the Old Testament experienced

The Doctrine Of Water Baptism

a typology of baptism. In the New Testament, John the Baptist, the forerunner of Christ and the Christian era, baptized seekers. Jesus submitted to the baptism of John, though John protested against Christ's need for baptism. Jesus taught, "… Except a man be born of water and of the Spirit, he cannot enter into the kingdom of God" (John 3:5). Jesus commanded his disciples to "Go ye therefore, and teach all nations, baptizing them in the name of the Father, and of the Son, and of the Holy Ghost: Teaching them to observe all things whatsoever I have commanded you…" (Matthew 28:19). The disciples of Christ baptized converts during Jesus' ministry. The apostles baptized converts into the church. No convert to Christianity recorded in the Scripture refused baptism.

Some treat baptism as an optional act we do because Christ saved us from our sins. Such terminology transcends into erroneous conclusions such as, "Since I am saved, why bother with baptism?" Contrary to the assumption of many, the Scripture associates baptism as a vital part of the new birth message. It isn't a ritual because one has experienced the new birth; it's part of the new birth process. Still, some delve into philosophical questions to discredit the significance of baptism. Here's a typical example: "If a candidate for baptism dies on his/her way to the baptistery, will he/she be lost for lack of baptism?" The issue is not how God judges the isolated cases; instead, the issue is whether or not we who minister to others, and those who desire Christianity, continue to follow the directives of Scripture regarding baptism. One of our best examples for this guideline is the biblical account of the Gentiles who received the Holy Spirit baptism before they experienced water baptism. Interestingly, the Apostle Peter commanded that they receive water baptism.

> While Peter yet spake these words, the Holy Ghost fell on all them which heard the word. And they of the circumcision which believed were astonished, as many as came with Peter, because that on the Gentiles also was poured out the gift of the Holy Ghost. For they heard them speak with tongues, and magnify God. Then answered Peter, Can any man forbid water, that these should not be baptized, which have received the Holy Ghost as well as we? And he commanded them to be baptized in the name of the Lord. Then prayed they him to tarry certain days.
>
> Acts 10:44-48

If baptism was not necessary, the apostle would not have insisted the Gentiles be baptized; contrariwise, he commanded their baptism, knowing full well he would have to answer to the

The Doctrine Of Water Baptism

Jewish church elders for accepting Gentiles into the Christian faith. The command and practice regarding baptism in the New Testament were never rescinded by the Scripture, nor do scriptural examples of conversions exempt anyone from baptism. Because the Scripture is our best guide for the Christian faith, and the Scripture undeniably teaches the necessity of baptism by commandment and by example, baptism should be a priority in every Christian church.

Who should be baptized?

When an individual believes that Jesus Christ is the Savior, and that individual has repented of sins and expressed faith in Jesus' atoning death to cover such sins, he/she is a candidate for baptism. No believer in Scripture was denied baptism. No repentant person is too bad to be denied baptism, nor can anyone be so good he/she should refuse baptism. The Apostle Peter, in his inaugural sermon at the birth of the church, and in response to the question regarding how to deal with one's sins, answered, "… Repent, and be baptized every one of you…" (Acts 2:38).

In order to conclude who should be baptized today, let's consider those who were baptized in the Scripture. First, we have examples of all nationalities being baptized: Jews (Acts 2); Samaritans (Acts 8:13); Gentiles (Acts 10:48). Second, individuals who were already very religious but who heard the message of the Christian faith accepted baptism. These included: Jewish priests (Acts 6:7); ordinary Jews who followed the strict Law of Moses (Acts 2:41); followers of John the Baptist who had already received baptism unto repentance, were re-baptized (Acts 19:1-5). Thirdly, no gender class precluded baptism: both males and females submitted to baptism. These examples represent all people of the entire world.

The question often arises, what is the appropriate age to baptize children? We have no reference in Scripture regarding the baptism of children. Therefore, it seems the age depends upon each child's ability to comprehend their need for baptism and their ability to comprehend and believe that Christ's atoning blood is applied to their sins at baptism. I vividly recall one case in point regarding a child's lack of understanding regarding baptism. The boy was about four years old, but he begged his mother to let him get baptized. So, his mother sat him down for a simple Bible lesson on baptism, explaining that at baptism all his sins would be forgiven, at which point he asked, "What sins?" She kindly nudged him to wait awhile for his baptism. He received baptism at a later date, and now in his thirties is still living for Christ. In this case the wait was probably the right decision.

The Doctrine Of Water Baptism

When should one be baptized?

From a scriptural perspective, baptism was administered as soon as one recognized himself to be a sinner, believed in Christ's atoning sacrifice for his sins, and repented of sins. Repentance has been described as an about-face from one's direction, desiring and committing to a changed lifestyle. There are four reasons for urgency in baptism. Let's consider each.

First, baptism signifies union with Christ in His redemptive act at Calvary. Baptism, coupled with a simple act of faith, produces monumental results. For whatever purpose God designed Calvary, baptism immediately applies that purpose to our lives. To be baptized is as if one is hanging alongside Christ on the cross and then buried alongside Him in His tomb. Baptism reflects two deaths: a negative and a positive. The negative reminds us that we are spiritually dead: because of Adam's transgression we inherit a sinful nature, and ultimately we commit personal sins. "Even when we were dead in sins ..." (Ephesians 2:5). The positive? Baptism is an acknowledgment that we are now dead to sin, but alive in Christ; therefore, we can now be an overcomer of sin. "How shall we, that are dead to sin, live any longer therein?" (Romans 6:2). Further, at baptism we are no longer indebted to sin, living under its condemnation. Baptism doesn't merely sweep our sins under the rug, hiding our past.

Through baptism into Christ, His sacrifice pays our debt of sin—Christ being the substitute for our death. Romans 6:3-4 states, "Know ye not, that so many of us as were baptized into Jesus Christ were baptized into his death? Therefore, we are buried with him by baptism into death … ." Baptism is a spiritual act that is symbolic of Christ's literal death, thus, at baptism, the wages of sin—death—is applied to us because of Christ's death. In that He was sinless and needed not to die, yet received the wages of sin, He allotted His death to apply to our debt.

Secondly, baptism signifies union with Christ's body—the church. "There is one body, and one Spirit, even as ye are called in one hope of your calling; One Lord, one faith, one baptism, One God and Father of all, who is above all, and through all, and in you all" (Ephesians 4:4-6). Baptism is a uniform act for all believers: as believers, we are one in Christ through the act of baptism. Random acts, without scriptural support, could bring confusion to the body of believers regarding their union in Christ. Baptism is a scripturally, consistent, and explicit teaching that establishes the means of individuals becoming a part of the Christian church.

Thirdly, baptism signifies entry into the spiritual Kingdom of God. It separates the church from all other social clubs: the church is a spiritual entity, described by Scripture as experiencing "… righteousness, and peace, and joy in the Holy Ghost" (Romans 14:17). Baptism is the act that

The Doctrine Of Water Baptism

separates true believers from acclaim seekers and window shoppers. Jesus said, "… Except a man be born of water and of the Spirit, he cannot enter into the kingdom of God" (John 3:5). Baptism (both by water and Spirit) is the door through which we enter into the Kingdom of God.

Finally, baptism signifies life in obedience to the rule of God. "Knowing this, that our old man is crucified with him, that the body of sin might be destroyed, that henceforth we should not serve sin. For he that is dead is freed from sin" (Romans 6:6-7). Why then should anyone who understands and desires salvation hesitate regarding baptism? There are key examples from Scripture that promote immediate baptism. The believers at Pentecost were baptized the same day: "Then they that gladly received his word were baptized: and the same day there were added unto them about three thousand souls" (Acts 2:41). The Philippian jailer and his entire household were baptized the same night of their conversion: "And he took them the same hour of the night, and washed their stripes; and was baptized, he and all his, straightway" (Acts 16:33).

Another example regarding immediate baptism is the Ethiopian eunuch: "And as they went on their way, they came unto a certain water: and the eunuch said, See, here is water; what doth hinder me to be baptized" (Acts 8:36)? These examples express expediency regarding baptism. There are no examples in Scripture suggesting postponing baptism for lack of necessity or out of inconvenience.

How should one be baptized?

There are two significant issues to consider regarding how we are to be baptized. One consideration is the physical manner of baptism? A second consideration is what words should the minister say at the baptism? First, let's consider the former issue: the physical manner of baptizing. Should the minister submerge the one being baptized? Or, as the custom of many, should the minister sprinkle or pour water on the head of the one being baptized? A simple study of the meaning of the English term "baptize" reveals the meaning as to "dip" or "plunge" instead of "sprinkle" or "pour."[4] The word itself, baptize, is one of those new words added to the English language. Instead of translating the word into English, the translators created a word from the old language. The meaning of the Greek word "baptizo" transliterated into English "baptize" bears out the physical manner used in reference to baptism—to dip or plunge: to submerge in water. Still, some argue that baptism does not have to be by submersion. Rather than delve into various essays on the subject, I prefer to consider some examples of New Testament Scripture regarding baptism. Without having to consult conflicting scholarly texts, a study of Scripture regarding Christian baptism definitely points to a pattern of submersion

The Doctrine Of Water Baptism

rather than sprinkling. Further, there is no biblical example supporting sprinkling or pouring.

References in the New Testament strongly support submersion as the proper means of Christian baptism:

- John chose a place where there was ample water to baptize: "And John also was baptizing in Aenon near to Salim, because there was much water there: and they came, and were baptized" (John 3:23). "And there went out unto him all the land of Judaea, and they of Jerusalem, and were all baptized of him in the river of Jordan, confessing their sins" (Mark 1:5).
- John baptized Jesus in the Jordan River, an indication of submersion. Christ is our ultimate example regarding baptism: "Then cometh Jesus from Galilee to Jordan unto John, to be baptized of him … And Jesus, when he was baptized, went up straightway out of the water …" (Matthew 3:13, 16).
- The account of the baptism of the Ethiopian indicates submersion: "And as they went on their way, they came unto a certain water: and the eunuch said, See, here is water; what doth hinder me to be baptized? And Philip said, If thou believest with all thine heart, thou mayest. And he answered and said, I believe that Jesus Christ is the Son of God. And he

commanded the chariot to stand still: and they went down both into the water, both Philip and the eunuch; and he baptized him. And when they were come up out of the water, the Spirit of the Lord caught away Philip, that the eunuch saw him no more: and he went on his way rejoicing" (Acts 8:36-39).

Let's reiterate two very important arguments supporting immersion. A study of the meaning of the English word "baptism" supports immersion. Biblical examples of Christian baptisms support submersion as the manner in which one should be baptized. There is no biblical reference for sprinkling as the manner for baptism. Sprinkling was a much later development, and historically, submersion seems to be the standard practice until about the twelfth century. Sprinkling seemed to come about for the sake of the sick, the aged, and for the convenience of another practice that lacks biblical support: infant baptism. Concerning infant baptism, we will discuss this in part five of this book.

The second issue regarding baptism is what words should the minister speak at the baptism ceremony. Many Christian churches baptize converts as they recite from instructions of Christ recorded by Matthew: "Go ye therefore, and teach all nations, baptizing them in the name of the Father, and of the Son, and of the Holy Ghost" (Matthew 28:19). Other Christian churches baptize converts

The Doctrine Of Water Baptism

reciting the instructions of Christ recorded by the gospel writer Luke: "And that repentance and remission of sins should be preached in his name among all nations, beginning at Jerusalem" (Luke 24:47). Both Scriptures have similarities: they are the instructions of Christ, they command the church to evangelize, and they instruct the disciples to baptize converts. However, some use Matthew's words as a formula for baptizing the convert into a Triune God, though Matthew declares no specific name; rather, he is vague regarding a name. Luke's directive is more specific, declaring the name of the Savior. An ongoing debate among Bible scholars is whether or not the Scripture, "Baptizing them in the name of the Father, and of the Son, and of the Holy Ghost" (Matthew 28:19) was altered by translators to accommodate the trinitarian doctrine that gained political favor in the early fourth century. Depending on whose research you read, arguments abound for and against. I chose not to include these scholarly debates in this book; instead, I point out there is absolutely no scriptural reference of a baptism to support the triune formula of baptism. Interestingly, multiple examples of baptisms in the Scripture follow Luke's directive: in or into the name of Jesus, the Lord, or Lord Jesus. Because of this overwhelming evidence of examples, and the many Scriptures that reference baptism as a union with Christ, the church should follow the directive of baptism in the name of Jesus as was set forth by the examples of Scripture.

A study of the examples of Christian baptism in the Scripture reveals that the name of Jesus as the Savior was always spoken at baptism. That is why many Christian ministers baptize converts by repeating this, or a similar, phrase: "Upon the confession of your sins and the profession of your faith, I baptize you in the name of the Lord Jesus Christ." There are three specific biblical commands fulfilled by this phrase:

- The demand for repentance to preface baptism is affirmed: "upon the confession of sin."
- The personal acknowledgment of ones' desire for salvation is expressed, and the belief that Jesus Christ is the Savior is affirmed: "the profession of your faith."
- The name and role of the Savior are specifically affirmed: by saying Lord, the individual now belongs to the God of Scripture; by saying Jesus, we are affirming that the monotheistic God of the Old Testament, Jehovah, has become our Savior; by saying Christ, we acknowledge Jesus as God Incarnate, the anointed of God for the purpose of mankind's redemption.

When the minister baptizes the believer while using the phrase "in the name of the Lord Jesus Christ," he denotes baptism's purpose: it is

The Doctrine Of Water Baptism

washing away one's sins by applying the atoning death of Jesus Christ, and the believer is entering into a relationship of belonging to Christ. John the Baptist's baptism incorporated the principles of repentance and acknowledgment of faith. However, John's baptism didn't introduce the convert to Christ as Lord and Savior. For this reason, we read the account in Scripture of disciples of John the Baptist who later converted to Christianity and were baptized a second time. Why? Paul instructed them to be baptized the second time, incorporating the name of the Savior at this second baptism. "Then said Paul, John verily baptized with the baptism of repentance, saying unto the people, that they should believe on him which should come after him, that is, on Christ Jesus. When they heard this, they were baptized in the name of the Lord Jesus" (Acts 19:4-5).

In contrast, the Christian baptism derived from Matthew's quotation of Christ does not incorporate the name of the Savior. Consider three reasons why the name of the Lord Jesus Christ should be called out at baptism:

- Jesus Christ is the Savior, and we are being baptized into Him (John 4:42; Galatians 3:27).
- We are commanded by Scripture to do all things in Jesus' name: all things including baptism (Acts 4:12; Colossians 3:17).

- Examples of baptism in Scripture were administered calling out the name of the Lord Jesus Christ.

With such scriptural references, is it not fitting that converts be baptized "in the name of Jesus Christ?"

Baptism into Christ is the purpose and means of atonement for sin.

Many do not realize the seriousness of sin: it is an offense to our Creator God because it is in direct opposition to what He is and to what He created us to be. Let me attempt to draw an analogy that may help describe sin's insult to God.

> A groom pays the entire expense to a beautiful resort in Hawaii for his lifelong friends who make up his wedding party: airplane tickets, motel, white tuxedos, spending money, with arrangements for an extended stay after the wedding. The day of the wedding, they do not show up, nor does his bride. He does not know what is going on until the exact hour the marriage is to begin, and his best man posts pictures on the Internet. His lifelong friends had gotten drunk at a bachelor party

The Doctrine Of Water Baptism

the night before the wedding—a party to which he had not been invited—and kidnapped his bride and enjoyed her company all night. Afterward, they strangled her and dumped her body in the ocean.

One cannot imagine the anguish, disbelief, dismay, and anger this groom would have experienced. Nor can we truly understand how God feels about sin: it is so opposite His nature. Oh, the anguish God must have felt when Adam and Eve, the greatest delight of His creation, listened to the deception of His greatest adversary and believed Satan instead of the God Who loved them. To add salt to injury, they tried to avoid Him in the garden.

Sin is not only an offense to God, but it also has both temporal and eternal consequences. The countless tragedies that happen every day reflect the temporal consequences of sin. Let us consider but one prime example. The Bible shares multiple warnings regarding drinking fermented wine. These warnings are extended to the numerous alcoholic drinks in which our society indulges, but mankind continues to ignore the warnings, and the result is tragic in many ways: death, disease, broken homes, poverty, perversion, et cetera. The world would be such a better place if we had not followed the shameful example Noah set before his sons. And so, the writer of Proverbs warned us of wine's consequences and commanded us to avoid such (Proverbs 4:17; 20:1; 21:17; 23:31; 31:4). With the track record of so many we know and love, we can readily see the temporal consequences of sin.

Further, the temporal consequences of sin culminate into the eternal, for the temporal consequences (no matter how harmful) do not negate the eternal consequences of sin (Luke 16:19-31). But God, in His great love for us, does not leave us hopelessly adrift on the raging sea of sin: He offers a remedy. Though we reap in this life what we sow, God offers a means to spare the individual from being eternally punished: atonement. And God's atoning plan is the only resolution for sin's eternal consequences. For sin to escape eternal consequences, it must be atoned for. And the Bible offers a specific atonement plan for sin.

In its ancient meaning, atonement denotes a uniting of severed relationships. As used in the Bible, it signifies reparation for a wrong. In the Old Testament, under the Mosaic practice, atonement consisted of sacrificial rituals, where slain animals substituted for mankind's sins. However, under this plan for atonement, the annual sacrifice merely pushed the day of reckoning forward and postponed the wrath of God in judgment against Israel as a nation. It is significant to consider that throughout the year, individuals also brought personal offerings for their sins. These, too, merely postponed God's judgment: the debt of sin was not sufficiently atoned

The Doctrine Of Water Baptism

for; thus condemnation remained.

Consider this definition of atonement: "To make an equivalent payment so that adequate recompense is made for an offense." The offense we are referencing? Sin. "For all have sinned, and come short of the glory of God" (Romans 3:23). Further, the Scripture declares, "… the wages of sin is death …" (Romans 6:23). Sin is horrendous, so much so that it corrupted a perfect creation: mankind was terribly changed from the perfection of his original state. And the cycle of sin continues into each new generation. The sinner works hard all his life; his wages for his life's work is death, then in the end, "… death and hell were cast into the lake of fire …" (Revelation 20:14). So, we need an equivalent payment for our sins—other than death—that is equivalent to death. But that is a quandary: there is no equivalent for death other than death. That is why, under the Mosaic plan, animals were sacrificed daily and annually. Still, the death of a creature—that had no knowledge of right and wrong, and which was created inferior to mankind—could not suffice for mankind's indebtedness to sin. God could have cast us off entirely into eternal damnation, but in His great mercy, He had already planned a remedy. That plan unfolded to mankind over time.

In the Old Testament, the Day of Atonement was the most important holy day of the Jewish year.

- It was a day of fasting, reflection upon and

confession of sins, and ultimately trusting that the Lord would accept the sacrifice offered by the priest for the sins of the nation.

- Two goats were presented to the high priest. He killed one and carried the blood into the inner Tabernacle—called the Holy of Holies because it represented God's presence. There he sprinkled the blood on the golden lid that covered the Ark of the Covenant, appropriately called the mercy seat. The Ark contained the tablets of the law, the primary Ten Commandments dictating how Israel should treat God and one another. The Mercy Seat, sprinkled with the blood of the sacrifice, stood between the wrath of God and the laws Israel had broken. The blood indicated that something (in this case, an animal) had paid the ultimate price—death—for the sins committed by the people. In retrospect, it is obvious the death of an animal was not equivalent to that of a human death; therefore, the debt of sin wasn't sufficiently paid, but God in His great grace postponed judgment until the next year.
- Each year the priests repeated this process, and each year God postponed judgment for Israel's sins. Because the sacrifice was temporary and insufficient, it had to be repeated the next year.
- After this sacrificial ritual with the first goat,

The Doctrine Of Water Baptism

the high priest placed his hands on the head of the second goat. This signified placing Israel's blame upon the goat, which was then led into the wilderness far away from the camp of Israel and released into the wild. This was symbolic of removing Israel's sins far away and thus postponing God's judgment.

If there was anything Israel learned about God in their wilderness wandering, it was that you follow His directives. They experienced firsthand that you don't make up your own agenda, pick and choose, or go for the convenient way. What about us? Is sin treated any differently? Is it any less offensive to God? Have we civilized ourselves into becoming a sinless society without the need for atonement? Or, like the nations adjoining Israel, can we simply call ourselves a non-covenant nation (non-Christian nation) and receive an exemption from the demands of the God of Christianity? The answer to these questions is an emphatic "no." All creation—every individual—must answer to the Creator, and all creation will be judged. All have sinned, and we all need a savior to atone for our sins. Jesus is that Savior. Calvary was designed by God as the only means of atonement for sin: past, present, and future.

At different eras in Scripture prior to Calvary, various means reflected God's accepted atonement, but atonement at any period of history always reflected the ultimate price: death. Such atonement began with Adam and Eve when God killed an animal and used the skin of the slain animal to cover their exposed bodies. As husband and wife, they did not need a covering for their nakedness, for no other humans existed at the time, so the animal skin was more than a covering for the body. It was symbolic of a covering for sin. Their disobedience had separated them from God, and His visitation with them ceased: God evidently withdrew from them because of their sinful nature. They needed atonement for their sin: a reuniting with God, reparation for the sin that distanced them from God.

Later, Adam and Eve's sons, Abel and Cain, likewise offered sacrifices: Abel offered a slain animal, and Cain brought fruit from his crops. God rejected Cain's sacrifice while accepting Abel's. In the process, Cain's true, sinful nature succumbed to jealousy, anger, and ultimately the murder of his brother. The sin of disobedience committed by Adam and Eve spiraled into murder by their son. Like a raging wildfire, sin never seems to be satisfied with its consumption of a person's activities. It always demands more.

We continue to see animal sacrifices during the age of the patriarchs—Abraham, Isaac, and Jacob. From Moses until Christ's ultimate sacrifice at Calvary, God demanded specifics regarding the sacrifices offered by His covenant people, Israel. Yet, all animal sacrifices were temporary, awaiting the Lamb prepared by God. And John affirmed

The Doctrine Of Water Baptism

such when he made the proclamation, "… Behold the Lamb of God, which taketh away the sin of the world" (John 1:29). The temporary sacrifices of the past became efficacious when Christ became the ultimate sacrifice.

The modern Christian community often overlooks Scriptures referencing atonement regarding sin. Many view the New Birth as merely a change of heart or turning over a new leaf. Conversely, obtaining New Testament salvation is much more than a denominational tradition or ritual. It is more than joining a church. There is a specific way in which our sins are atoned.

With the old sacrificial system no longer in effect—replaced and fulfilled by Christ's atoning sacrifice at Calvary—how do we apply Christ's sacrifice to our sins? The biblical directive to identify with the atonement made by Christ at Calvary is through baptism into Christ. I like the clarity with which The Message interpretation of Scripture speaks regarding baptism:

> So what do we do? Keep on sinning so God can keep on forgiving? I should hope not! If we've left the country where sin is sovereign, how can we still live in our old house there? Or didn't you realize we packed up and left there for good? That is what happened in baptism. When we went

under the water, we left the old country of sin behind; when we came up out of the water, we entered into the new country of grace—a new life in a new land! That's what baptism into the life of Jesus means. When we are lowered into the water, it is like the burial of Jesus; when we are raised up out of the water, it is like the resurrection of Jesus. Each of us is raised into a light-filled world by our Father so that we can see where we're going in our new grace-sovereign country.

Romans 6:1-5[5]

Baptism is both the example and message of Christ. Christ submitted to baptism for our example, not because He had sinned. Further, He preached baptism for all converts. He instructed His disciples to baptize believers. Because of Christ's teaching, baptism was the message and practice of the apostles and the first church. This is recorded in Scripture. It is not an optional message regarding salvation, nor is it merely a suggestion. It is the command of Christ, and it comes with the promise of Christ: "He that believeth and is baptized shall be saved; but he that believeth not shall be damned" (Mark 16:16). "Jesus answered, Verily, verily, I say unto thee, Except a man be born of water and of the Spirit, he cannot enter into the kingdom of God" (John 3:5).

The Doctrine Of Water Baptism

Some suggest Christ's teaching wasn't speaking of water baptism; rather, they say it was speaking of water associated with one's natural birth. This seems a far-fetched explanation: especially since all scriptural references to the new birth include water baptism. Further, no convert to the New Testament church refused baptism, thus fulfilling the command of Scripture for baptism and affirming its significance. All examples of conversions include water baptism, and the Scripture associates baptism with applying Christ's death as atonement for our sins: it's as if we die because of our sins, but instead, Jesus took our place. And just how does that work? He applies His death to our sins at baptism: "Buried with him in baptism…" (Colossians 2:12). Simply put, Christ proclaims our sins atoned for when we receive His sacrificial gift by identifying with His death through water baptism.

Part Five
Questions Regarding Baptism

For as many of you as have been
baptized into Christ have put on Christ.
Galatians 3:27

The accounts of scriptural baptisms in the first church reflect baptism into Jesus Christ. A question arises: What about Jesus' command in Matthew 28:19 to baptize converts into the titles: father, son, and Holy Ghost? Isn't this a direct command of Christ? Let us consider this Scripture and compare it with like-minded Scriptures. This will explain how the Apostles carried out the command to baptize converts in the name of the Father, and of the Son, and of the Holy Ghost as they baptized in the name of the Lord Jesus Christ. A corresponding command of Jesus regarding baptism was recorded by Luke:

> And said unto them, Thus it is written,
> and thus it behooved Christ to suffer,
> and to rise from the dead the third day:

> And that repentance and remission
> of sins should be preached in his
> name among all nations, beginning
> at Jerusalem. And ye are witnesses of
> these things.
>
> Luke 24:46-48

"Baptism into the name" indicates that the baptized person is closely bound to, or is the property of, the one into whose name he is baptized. The apostles spoke the name of Jesus at baptism, signifying their understanding of Who Jesus was and what His name represented. "Then Peter said unto them, Repent, and be baptized every one of you in the name of Jesus Christ for the remission of sins… (Acts 2:38)."

Both Scripture and history affirm that the early church used Jesus' name in baptism. A host of historical references acknowledge the teaching of baptism in Jesus' name is not a new doctrine; rather, it was an acceptable practice in antiquity. Here's an example of an archived historical explanation, *An Encyclopedia of Religions, by Maurice A. Canney,* regarding baptism in Jesus' name as the original mode of baptism:

> Persons were baptized at first "in the
> name of Jesus Christ" (Acts ii. 38, x.
> 48) or "in the name of the Lord Jesus"
> (Acts viii. Ifi, xix. 5). Afterwards, with

Questions Regarding Baptism

the development of the doctrine of the Trinity, they were baptized "in the name of the Father and of the Son and of the Holy Ghost" (cp. Justin Martyr, Apol. i.61.[6]

This is but one of several examples of historical evidence of the first church baptizing in the name of the Lord Jesus. However, I have chosen to focus on the biblical narrative of baptism instead of the historical. This tends to be the safest way. Three of the gospel writers emphasized the significance of the spoken Words of Christ: "Heaven and earth shall pass away, but my words shall not pass away" (Matthew 24:25; Mark 13:31; Luke 21:33). Examples of obedience to Christ by the disciples regarding baptism are recorded in the Acts of the Apostles. These are ample biblical examples of baptism to conclude that the early church baptized converts in the name of the Lord Jesus Christ.

The command for baptism recorded by Matthew states "baptizing in the name." He did not say baptize in the names, rather, name—singular. Some suggest this explanation as being unscholarly, but the Bible has always emphasized the name of God. Individuals sought out the name of God. Angels proclaimed the name of God. Prayers in Scripture were directed to God using a specific name. We can readily admit that God is not the name of our God; rather, God is Who He is in relationship to us. Likewise, son is not a name, and Holy Ghost is not God's name. These are titles that represent God, but they are not His name. Considering the emphasis that is placed upon the name of the God of Scripture, should we not use a specific name for such a serious act as baptism? That is why we should call the name of Jesus at baptism. Jesus is the name of God Incarnate: God with us. Not only is Jesus the name of the Savior, the meaning of the name incorporates the name of the God of the Old Testament. Jesus' name by definition means "Jehovah has become salvation."

Further, Jesus said, "I am come in my father's name" (John 5:43). Jesus' name was not a random selection by His parents; rather, it was God's selection, and God dispatched an angel that announced specifically, "... thou shalt call his name Jesus: for he shall save his people from their sins" (Matthew 1:21). This proclamation was a fulfillment of the Old Testament prophet's decree, "Now all this was done, that it might be fulfilled which was spoken of the Lord by the prophet, saying, Behold, a virgin shall be with child, and shall bring forth a son, and they shall call his name Emmanuel, which being interpreted is, God with us" (Matthew 1:22-23). This latter Scripture affirms the former: Jesus is the Incarnate God of the Old Testament. And the saving name God chose is Jesus: an extension of an Old Testament name for God. Finally, the Scripture shows in various translations that the examples of baptism in the first church were done in the name of

Questions Regarding Baptism

Jesus, Jesus Christ, Lord, or Lord Jesus (Acts 2:38; 8:16; 10:48; 19:5). The New International Version of Scripture specifically uses Jesus in all four of these scriptural references. The Apostle Peter further expressed, "Neither is there salvation in any other: for there is none other name under heaven given among men, whereby we must be saved" (Acts 4:12).

There are a few baptisms recorded in the Scripture that do not share the specifics of the baptism ceremony: Lydia and her household (Acts 16:15); the Philippian jailer and his household (Acts 16:25-33); Paul (Acts 9:18). But of these three, we have significant insight into the jailer's and Paul's conversions. Consider the events that took place just before the baptism of the jailer:

> And at midnight Paul and Silas prayed, and sang praises unto God: and the prisoners heard them. And suddenly there was a great earthquake, so that the foundations of the prison were shaken: and immediately all the doors were opened, and every one's bands were loosed. And the keeper of the prison awaking out of his sleep, and seeing the prison doors open, he drew out his sword, and would have killed himself, supposing that the prisoners had been fled. But Paul cried with

a loud voice, saying, Do thyself no harm: for we are all here. Then he called for a light, and sprang in, and came trembling, and fell down before Paul and Silas, And brought them out, and said, Sirs, what must I do to be saved? And they said, Believe on the Lord Jesus Christ, and thou shalt be saved, and thy house. And they spake unto him the word of the Lord, and to all that were in his house. And he took them the same hour of the night, and washed their stripes; and was baptized, he and all his, straightway. And when he had brought them into his house, he set meat before them, and rejoiced, believing in God with all his house.

Acts 16:25-34

In this dialog, a criterion for salvation included believing upon the Lord Jesus Christ: a specific name regarding salvation. And the Scripture paints a scene of the entire household being baptized immediately after this confession of faith.

In considering Paul's baptism, two things are noteworthy: one is from the personal testimony of his baptism, and the other is from his comments in a letter to the church at Corinth. Let's consider each. First, when Paul recounts his baptism experience, he points out that Ananias called out the name of

Questions Regarding Baptism

the Lord at his baptism: "And now why tarriest thou? arise, and be baptized, and wash away thy sins, calling on the name of the Lord" (Acts 22:16). In Paul's letter to the church at Corinth, when addressing the division among the church members because of their preference for a particular minister, he makes an interesting observation:

> For it hath been declared unto me of you, my brethren, by them which are of the house of Chloe, that there are contentions among you. Now this I say, that every one of you saith, I am of Paul; and I of Apollos; and I of Cephas; and I of Christ. Is Christ divided? was Paul crucified for you? or were ye baptized in the name of Paul? I thank God that I baptized none of you, but Crispus and Gaius; Lest any should say that I had baptized in mine own name.
>
> I Corinthians 1:11-15

In this passage of Scripture we see the significance of a specific name regarding baptism. In writing to the Galatian church—who had somewhat lapsed into Judaism, as if that gave them preference with God—Paul expressed that being Jewish or Greek had no significance in the Kingdom of God, for it was baptism into Christ that was significant:

> For ye are all the children of God by
> faith in Christ Jesus. For as many of you
> as have been baptized into Christ have
> put on Christ. There is neither Jew nor
> Greek, there is neither bond nor free,
> there is neither male nor female: for ye
> are all one in Christ Jesus. And if ye be
> Christ's, then are ye Abraham's seed,
> and heirs according to the promise.
>
> Galatians 3:26-29

Many are quick to point out that their beloved grandma wasn't baptized "in Jesus name" but was a godly person in love with Christ, using this reference to refute the significance of Jesus' name baptism. The issue isn't about a deceased grandparent or the host of scenarios offered; the issue is a search of truth for the here and now. What does the Bible say for us today? What is the message that we need to teach and practice? Should we baptize according to Scripture or tradition? Should we follow the example of the apostles in the first church, or should we follow the example of family and their religious traditions?

Some erroneously perceive that Calvary is but one of many ways into heaven. This conclusion is drawn somewhat due to the various dispensations in the Bible, when salvation did not include baptism into Christ. A dispensation is a time period in which God revealed a specific doctrine which was practiced

Questions Regarding Baptism

by the believers of that day. These dispensations included various means by which mankind obtained salvation: they offered sacrifices, they built a boat, they participated in the rite of circumcision, or they obeyed a list of rules. We conclude that without baptism into Christ they were still saved. Some take this concept a step farther, arguing that neither do we need to be baptized into Christ today. They conclude that one can obtain salvation through various means: confess our sins, acknowledge Christ as Savior, turn over a new leaf. The Bible, however, is much more specific than this; therefore, we should look to the Scripture for details.

A closer study of Scripture reveals the far-reaching influence the crucified Christ would have in the lives of those of past dispensations. From Adam until the present, the only means into the Kingdom of God is the sacrifice of Christ. How can this be? Calvary's sacrifice, though it occurred at a specific time in history, was not limited to that specific time period. The sacrifice at Calvary applied to past, present, and future generations. So, in dispensations before Calvary, God gave unique stipulations whereby Calvary (which was to come) would apply to an individual's life.

The message of Good Friday is much more than a holiday; it is the only hope of humanity: past, present, and future. Anything less than Christ's redemptive plan is inadequate to remove the curse of sin. Adam and Eve sinned and therefore disseminated the seed of corruption to all humanity, eternally separating us from God. Though mankind did not have the means to regain the position with God that he enjoyed in the garden, God planned a way to get His creation back to Him. Not only did God have a plan, God's plan predated humanity's creation. Before the creation, God, in His omniscience, recognized that Adam would fail; therefore, God envisioned a Savior: a substitute sacrifice for humankind's future sin. "That it might be fulfilled which was spoken by the prophet, saying, I will open my mouth in parables; I will utter things which have been kept secret from the foundation of the world" (Matthew 13:35). John, the writer of Revelation, shares a date of the crucifixion that conflicts with the actual timeline of events. "And all that dwell upon the earth shall worship him, whose names are not written in the book of life of the Lamb slain from the foundation of the world" (Revelation 13:8). Calvary and the struggle in the Garden of Gethsemane predated the garden of Eden and mankind's fall. John also wrote, "In the beginning was the Word ..." (John 1:1). This Word (or the Greek term, Logos) was the thought or the plan of God for a fallen humanity long before Adam and Eve failed. God envisioned their Savior before He created Adam and Eve. "And the Word was made flesh..." (John 1:14). God's planned redeemer for fallen humanity—another man— was Jesus Christ. He was God Incarnate, or God in human flesh. Jesus became more than a thought when God took a human form in a virgin's womb. The purpose of that human flesh was to become the sacrificial lamb of God for all mankind. Paul called Jesus the second Adam (1 Corinthians 15:45), but Jesus existed in God's plan before the first Adam was formed. In contrast to how we sometimes perceive Jesus and Adam, Jesus wasn't formed from the image of Adam; rather, God formed Adam according to the image He had of the redeemer—the Logos—before humanity existed. "Nevertheless death reigned from Adam to Moses, even over them that had not sinned after the similitude of Adam's transgression, who is the figure of him that was to come" (Romans 5:14). Did you catch that? Adam was the image of Him that was to come: Adam was the image of Christ. The Savior and Calvary and mankind's redemption were prophetically planned before mankind sinned.

The light of creation illuminated the cross more than the cosmos, casting its shadow onto a lowly manger. Calvary loomed in the corner of a stable where a baby wept, awaiting the maturity of the infant and the cry from Gethsemane's Garden, "…thy will be done" (Matthew 26:42). The hope of all humanity before Calvary, and all humanity after Calvary, was and is in the cross of Jesus. Those before Calvary sought redemption in obedient faith to God's demands of sacrifice. Though bloodied by the rite of circumcision and animal sacrifices, the Jewish priests were indifferent to the big picture: salvation would come through the sacrifice of the Lamb of God. The message of Calvary slowly unfolded as mankind brought substitute, animal sacrifices and slaughtered them on altars of repentance. Each of these was meaningless were it not for the coming slaughter of Christ at Golgotha. Beginning with Abraham, the Jewish people incorporated the ritual of circumcision, a typology of separation from sin and the cutting away of sinful flesh. This, too, was but a bloody mess without the planned shedding of Christ's blood to separate mankind from his sins. With Moses, there began codified and precise statutes of law given from atop Sinai, including a continuance of circumcision and animal sacrifices. In retrospect, the writer of the New Testament Book of Hebrews explains that all the countless sacrifices of the Old Testament were meaningless without the coming sacrifice of Christ: fulfilled when He died on the cross.

> The Holy Ghost this signifying, that the way into the holiest of all was not yet made manifest, while as the first tabernacle was yet standing: Which was a figure for the time then present, in which were offered both gifts and sacrifices, that could not make him that did the service perfect, as pertaining to the conscience; Which stood only in meats and drinks, and divers washings,

and carnal ordinances, imposed on them until the time of reformation. But Christ being come an high priest of good things to come, by a greater and more perfect tabernacle, not made with hands, that is to say, not of this building; Neither by the blood of goats and calves, but by his own blood he entered in once into the holy place, having obtained eternal redemption for us.

Hebrews 9:8-12

The writer to the Hebrew Christians expressed concern that they held too tightly to the Old Covenant and traditions. He explained that the annual rituals of the Old Testament were but a prototype of the planned sacrifice to come:

For the law having a shadow of good things to come, and not the very image of the things, can never with those sacrifices which they offered year by year continually make the comers thereunto perfect. For then would they not have ceased to be offered? because that the worshippers once purged should have had no more conscience of sins. But in those sacrifices there is a remembrance again made of sins

every year. For it is not possible that
the blood of bulls and of goats should
take away sins.

Hebrews 10:1-4

The provision for forgiveness of sin under the
Old Covenant could be compared to using a modern-
day credit system, knowing full well that payment
must eventually be made. But a spiritually bankrupt
humanity had no means of making payment for their
debt of sin. However, Christ's death at Calvary paid
the debt incurred even in the past: His blood flowed
backward, all the way to the gates of the forbidden
garden from which mankind had been cast out.

But what about those who live after Calvary.
Post-calvary ushered in prepaid credit cards (this is
not to suggest one iota that we are free to sin because
we have a get-out-of-jail-free card). We who live
after Calvary's sacrifice, who accept Christ from a
biblical perspective of the New Birth, draw from the
reserves deposited at Calvary almost two thousand
years ago. Though Calvary appeared at a specific
time in history, Christ's sacrifice paid the debt of
sinners in the past, present, and future. This was the
message the Apostle Peter—the one to whom Christ
gave the keys to the Kingdom of Heaven—preached
at the birth of the church.

For David speaketh concerning him,
I foresaw the Lord always before my

Questions Regarding Baptism

face, for he is on my right hand, that I should not be moved: Therefore did my heart rejoice, and my tongue was glad; moreover also my flesh shall rest in hope: Because thou wilt not leave my soul in hell, neither wilt thou suffer thine Holy One to see corruption. Thou hast made known to me the ways of life; thou shalt make me full of joy with thy countenance. Men and brethren, let me freely speak unto you of the patriarch David, that he is both dead and buried, and his sepulchre is with us unto this day. Therefore being a prophet, and knowing that God had sworn with an oath to him, that of the fruit of his loins, according to the flesh, he would raise up Christ to sit on his throne; He seeing this before spake of the resurrection of Christ, that his soul was not left in hell, neither his flesh did see corruption. This Jesus hath God raised up, whereof we all are witnesses. Therefore being by the right hand of God exalted, and having received of the Father the promise of the Holy Ghost, he hath shed forth this, which ye now see and hear. For David is not ascended into the heavens: but he saith himself, The Lord said unto my Lord, Sit thou on my right hand, Until I make thy foes thy footstool. Therefore let all the house of Israel know assuredly, that God hath made the same Jesus, whom ye have crucified, both Lord and Christ. Now when they heard this, they were pricked in their heart, and said unto Peter and to the rest of the apostles, Men and brethren, what shall we do? Then Peter said unto them, Repent, and be baptized every one of you in the name of Jesus Christ for the remission of sins, and ye shall receive the gift of the Holy Ghost. For the promise is unto you, and to your children, and to all that are afar off, even as many as the LORD our God shall call.

Acts 2:25-39[7]

For us living some two-thousand years removed from Christ's death, we must look backward to Calvary. To acknowledge the event of the crucifixion of Christ and to express faith in the cross is necessary, but we also need to personally identify with that long-ago event. The scriptural manner in which we identify with Christ's death, and cause Christ's death to apply to our debt of sin, is through baptism into Christ! And Christ's death is sufficient to pay the debt for all our sins. The Bible states,

Questions Regarding Baptism

"In fact, the law requires that nearly everything be cleansed with blood, and without the shedding of blood there is no forgiveness" (Hebrews 9:22 NIV). The entirety of Scripture points to Calvary, to Christ's shed blood. There are numerous references to the blood shedding of Christ, and each is a sign of hope for sinful mankind:

- Eight days after Christ's birth (circumcision): The wounding of the body, a typology of the cutting away of sinful flesh and the renunciation of the sins of the flesh, was a sign of hope. The priest asked Mary and Joseph, "What shall we call Him?" Joseph's response? "Jesus." Jehovah Savior. The angel had already announced, "Call Him Jesus, for He shall save His people from their sins."
- The agony in the garden: Jesus prayed so intently, asking that Calvary be bypassed, that His sweat became as great drops of blood. He was so exhausted and overwhelmed that an angel came and ministered to him, but God refused to change the plan. There was no other plan for mankind's salvation. It was the Logos of God—prearranged for mankind's redemption. God Himself would be born of a virgin, without sin, and He would shed His innocent blood to pay mankind's debt of sin.
- Scourging by the Romans: God does not waste suffering. He proclaimed, "… by whose

stripes ye were healed" (I Peter 2:24). "… all things work together for good…" (Romans 8:28).

- The crown of thorns: Pilate had the soldiers attach to the cross a sign proclaiming Christ to be "King of the Jews." The crowning with thorns was done in mockery by the soldiers, but symbolically it was a message that even Pilate, though pressed by the Jewish authorities, refused to revoke.

- Crucifixion: Jesus prayed, "… Father, forgive them; for they know not what they do …" (Luke 23:34). The mob was not aware that their cruel act was the plan of God— it was purchasing their own salvation and the salvation of all mankind past, present, and future. The priests of the Old Covenant bore the blood of sacrificial animals into the Tabernacle. When Christ—our high priest— appeared before the eternal Judge, He did not carry the blood of an animal sacrificed for mankind's sins, He carried His own sinless blood. "Take heed therefore unto yourselves, and to all the flock, over the which the Holy Ghost hath made you overseers, to feed the church of God, which he hath purchased with his own blood" (Acts 20:28).

- Piercing of the heart: When the Roman soldier thrust his spear into the heart of Christ, the veil in the temple was rent from top to bottom,

Questions Regarding Baptism

an act performed by the hand of God. As the point of the spear pierced the heart, a shaft split through the tombs and sarcophaguses of Old Testament saints, and many arose from the dead as a witness of God's power of redemption—the blood flowed backward. The event was affirmed by the non-believing and callused Roman soldiers when in amazement one proclaimed, "Truly this was the son of God" (Matthew 27:54).

Forty days after Christ's birth, His parents presented Him to the temple priests in accordance with Jewish law that the firstborn belongs to the Lord. With this act His parents sealed His destination, for the Lord had Calvary in mind, and nothing (not the goodness, the faithfulness, and the unearned shame and pain Calvary brought personally to the sinless Christ) would stop God's plan of a "… Lamb slain from the foundation of the world" (Revelation 13:8). God had us in mind, all mankind in mind, when He arranged for His Lamb to be born. Our only hope of redemption was Christ's sacrificial death. When Christ died, Adam and Eve's debt of sin was stamped "paid in full." Further, Abraham's lie was forgiven; Moses murder was erased; David, who wrote "… thou wilt not leave my soul in hell …" (Psalms 16:10), was released from his guilt of adultery and murder. Christ's blood flowed backward and forward. In retrospect, each period of time had a unique means of identifying with Christ's death: Adam to Noah; Noah to Abraham; Abraham to Moses. Before the Mosaic Law there existed a moral and social conscience, a loose set of oral guidelines. A non-uniform ritual of animal sacrifices directed the believers of the monotheistic God. Some twenty-five hundred years into man's existence, God gave to Moses a codified set of Commandments and a uniform sacrificial system with stringent guidelines. Looking forward, during the great tribulation and with the absence of the Christian ministry, Christ's sacrifice is applied to individuals as they choose death by martyrdom for refusing to take the mark of the beast. For us today, the advent of Calvary is applied by obedience to water baptism in the name of Jesus. When we are baptized into Christ, His blood flows forward from two millenniums past and washes away all our sins.

What about Paul's statement regarding baptism? "For Christ sent me not to baptize, but to preach the gospel ..." (I Corinthians 1:17).

This statement is in the opening chapter of Paul's letter to the church at Corinth. To correctly understand the meaning of this Scripture, we must understand its context. A good rule for Bible interpretation is to ask, "What is the subject of the Scripture?" This helps to prevent us from isolating a Scripture and improperly interpreting its meaning.

Questions Regarding Baptism

In following this rule of interpretation, we find the subject of this Scripture was not baptism; instead, the subject was an issue regarding unity. Here is the Scripture in its more complete context:

> For it hath been declared unto me of you, my brethren, by them which are of the house of Chloe, that there are contentions among you. Now this I say, that every one of you saith, I am of Paul; and I of Apollos; and I of Cephas; and I of Christ. Is Christ divided? was Paul crucified for you? or were ye baptized in the name of Paul? I thank God that I baptized none of you, but Crispus and Gaius; Lest any should say that I had baptized in mine own name. And I baptized also the household of Stephanas: besides, I know not whether I baptized any other.
>
> I Corinthians 1:11-16

The church at Corinth had splintered into factions, and it seems these factions had to do somewhat with who had baptized them. Paul's challenge reminds them there is only one Savior: Jesus. None of the personalities mentioned died for them except Jesus. Also, the Scripture promotes the idea of baptism into a name; further, the Scripture proclaims the name of Jesus as the only name sufficient to save. Paul further reflects, that because the contention was so great among the Corinthian church, if he had baptized very many converts, he might have been accused by some of baptizing them as personal converts unto himself: in his own name. His conclusion, he was glad he had personally baptized but a few of them. So, his statement "… Christ sent me not to baptize, but to preach the gospel …" was not intended to minimize the significance of baptism; contrariwise, the fact that baptism had created such an issue of division speaks of its impact upon the life of a believer. Let's consider six points regarding this verse:

- Paul himself was baptized (Acts 9:17-18).
- Paul named some whom he remembered personally baptizing (I Corinthians 1:14-16).
- Many were baptized at Corinth during Paul's ministry (Acts 18:8-11).
- Paul's primary contribution to the Corinthians was his teaching: "And he continued there a year and six months, teaching the word of God among them" (Acts 18:11).
- We can assume from the account of his letter to the Corinthians, and the documentation in the Book of Acts of his ministry at Corinth, that many were baptized. I believe it is a fair assumption that Paul did the preaching, and his associates did the baptizing. After all, we understand from Scripture that Paul suffered

some type of infirmity, which may have affected his ability to perform physical tasks.

- In Luke's chronicle of Paul's missionary journey, Paul left Corinth and went to Ephesus, where he met disciples of John the Baptist. He spoke to them regarding their previous baptism by John, and they submitted to baptism a second time, but this time they were baptized in the name of the Lord Jesus (Acts 19:1-7).

From these examples, we can deduce that Paul absolutely believed and preached the necessity of baptism.

What about infant baptism?

We have no biblical example for infant baptism, and rightly so, for an infant cannot confess sin, express faith, nor make a personal decision regarding baptism. Many churches practice an infant dedication, which does have biblical support; however, an infant dedication is asking God's blessing upon the child, not God's forgiveness nor regeneration, as the child is in a state of innocence.

Historical accounts place the practice of infant baptism as beginning around the third century. An article in Biblical Archaeological Review suggests infant baptism came about at a desperate time for parents who saw their children dying from a pandemic: the Antonine Plague, which killed as many as twenty percent of the population of the Roman Empire. Once the pandemic passed, the practice of infant baptism remained and became common within the church.[8]

What about baptism in the name of Yeshua instead of Jesus?

Some proponents of Christian baptism insist upon using the Hebrew name of Jesus at baptism, arguing that the English name, Jesus, derived from the Latin, Ἰησοῦς, or from the Greek, *Iēsoûs*, is insufficient to remit one's sins. Because of such insistence by some to use the Hebraic language, I believe it incumbent upon those who teach baptism in Jesus' name to answer such a challenge. Let's consider when and how this teaching came about. In so doing, we can realize the teaching of the *Yeshua* movement is scripturally unfounded regarding baptism. And it certainly should not be imposed on English-speaking Christians.

In the early nineteen-hundreds, the *Sacred Name Movement* (SNM) attempted to return Christianity to its Jewish roots. They translated the Bible using what they considered to be proper Hebrew names for God. They used *Yahweh* in the Old Testament for the name of God and *Yahshua* in the New Testament for Jesus—though some scholars refute this spelling, contending it should be *Yeshua,* thus

Questions Regarding Baptism

I will use this spelling. Proponents of this doctrine insisted that the Hebrew name, *Yeshua*, instead of the English, Jesus, be used at Christian baptism. However, the insistence on using *Yeshua* instead of Jesus for English speaking believers is without biblical or scholarly support. While baptism in the name of *Yeshua* is undoubtedly an acceptable mode of baptism when one is speaking Hebrew, it is not necessary for English speaking ministers to say the Hebrew name for Jesus in order for the baptism to be valid. Let's consider why it is proper for English speaking Christians to use the name Jesus when referencing the Savior.

My North American, English-speaking mother gave me the name Larry, but had she been Latino, she may have called me *Lorencito*. The names are the same: one is English, the other is Spanish. Whether one is speaking in Spanish or English is the determining factor as to which pronunciation will be used. Likewise, when you say Jesus, you are saying the name of the Savior, but you are speaking it in English, not Hebrew. A simple comparison would be the various colors. The colors are the same in all languages but with different names. No matter what language you use when describing the color of the sky, it is the same color seen by all people of every language: blue—if you describe it in the English language. Whether you say *pala* in the Luangiua language, *niebieski* in the Polish language, or *modro* in the Romani language, you are speaking of the same color: blue.

The Hebrew name *Yeshua*, or its derivatives, have a specific meaning: "the Lord is salvation" or "Jehovah has become our Savior." Likewise, to use the English name, Jesus, the meaning remains the same: the name is associated with God bringing salvation to mankind through His Incarnation. Both the Hebrew and Greek names for Jesus were used during the first century—ancient documents prove such. At the baptism of a Hebrew speaking convert to Christianity, the Hebrew language (Aramaic) would have been used. *Yeshua* was probably the name of choice by first-century Hebrews. Still, when the apostle Peter preached to Cornelius' and his household, he would have conversed in the universal language of the Roman Empire: Greek. This common language, sometimes called the market language, is referred to as the lingua franca of his day ("… a language or dialect systematically used to make communication possible between people who do not share a native language or dialect, particularly when it is a third language that is distinct from both native languages…").[9]

This universal, Grecian dialect dominated the New Testament church that became scattered across the Roman Empire, even though the Romans—whose official language was Latin—remained the ruling power for centuries. The Roman Empire had followed the influential Classical Greek period (776-323 BC) which flourished when Alexander the

Questions Regarding Baptism

Great conquered the world. As part of Alexander's strategy, he sent teachers to spread the Greek culture and language. Though the Romans conquered the Greeks after Alexander's death, they never cast off the Grecian influence throughout the world. It was the Roman army that dominated the world during the early church, but everywhere you looked, you saw the impact of the Grecian culture: architecture, philosophy, religion, and language. All of civilization spoke some form of a Grecian dialect. When the followers of Jesus carried the gospel to the known world, they traversed cobblestone roads that connected to Rome, but they conversed in a language linked to Athens. Referred to as Koine Greek, it "… arose as a common dialect within the armies of Alexander the Great …. It replaced existing ancient Greek dialects with an everyday form that people anywhere could understand."[10] So, the Apostle Peter probably preached to Cornelius and his household in this common language, not Hebrew. He baptized them, probably pronouncing the name *Iēsoûs*, which was the Greek form of the name of *Yeshua*.

In translation, to keep a text pure to its original form, it is sometimes necessary to transliterate certain words instead of interpreting the meaning. Transliteration is done by creating a like-minded word corresponding with the language you are translating from. In his book, *The Messiah's Name: Jesus, Not Yahshua*, Daniel L. Seagraves states: "Actually, to transliterate is to preserve the pronunciation of words as closely as possible from one language to another."[11] Since the entire Roman Empire spoke Greek, not only had the Old Testament been translated into the Greek language around the third to the first century BC (called the Septuagint), but most of the New Testament was originally written in the Greek language; thus the Hebrew name for Jesus was transliterated into its Greek form. Later, the Greek name took on a Latin form, Ἰησοῦς (especially as the Roman church dominated Christianity). Ultimately, the Latin form of the Greek name for Jesus (*Iēsoûs*) was transliterated into English, which is Jesus. This English transliteration is spelled and spoken similarly to the original Greek writing of the New Testament.

Some suggest the Greek form of Jesus, *Iēsoûs*, is of pagan influence (after the Greek God, Zeus, Ζεύς). Contrarywise, *Iēsoûs*, for various reasons, is not of pagan influence: the Greek names (*Iēsoûs*, Jesus, and Ζεύς, Zeus) are different in both spelling and pronunciation. Further, they are of different origins. Working backwards, the English name, Jesus, is a derivative of the Greek, *Iēsoû*, which is derived from the Hebrew, *Yeshua*, which is of the ancient Hebrew religion. In contrast, the English name, Zeus, is derived from the Greek, Ζεύς, which is derived from classical mythology.

As previously used in an analogy, just as we translate the color of the sky into various languages,

Questions Regarding Baptism

it is proper to translate *Yeshua* into all languages. Further, it is appropriate for that translation to be used in prayer, praise, and baptism. For English speaking nations, Jesus is the accepted name of God Incarnate, the Savior of the world. Let's consider three arguments of why baptism in the name of Jesus is valid for English speaking converts to Christianity.

First, let's consider in greater depth how we arrive at baptism in Jesus name instead of the Hebrew name *Yeshua*. Since I am not a language scholar, I must rely upon the shared, collective knowledge of linguistic scholars regarding the English translation of Scripture. One such scholarly study on this subject is a book I previously quoted from and recommend, written by Danial L. Seagraves.[12] Though there are disputations among scholars, there is a commonality to which they have arrived. The commonly held information regarding the New Testament is that the original manuscripts were written in the standard universal language of that day: Greek. Though there are some who suggest the original Gospel of Matthew was written in Hebrew, the oldest known fragments and copies of the New Testament are all written in Greek. We can reason that the transcribers of the New Testament used the Greek translation of the Hebrew name for the Savior: *Iēsoûs*. In later times, the English translators of Scripture made a choice to use the Greek name for the Savior (not the Hebrew) and transliterated it into

English. To transliterate a name is to use the same name of a language but adapt it with the alphabet of the language into which it is being translated. The English translators gave the Greek name an English spelling and pronunciation (very similar to the Greek in spelling and pronunciation). They simply chose to transliterate the Greek name for Jesus instead of using the Hebrew name. Why? I assume that to insert Hebrew names into a Greek translation would not have been in harmony with the rest of the translation. Likewise, if the English translators had translated the Hebrew name of Jesus into English, the name could have been Joshua instead of Jesus. It indeed would not have remained *Yeshua*. In short, since the oldest known copies of the New Testament were in Greek, and had been popularized into Latin, the English translators used the translated name, which became Jesus. It was a matter of choice that made perfect sense and maintained consistency in translation. But note again, the translators had no Hebrew, New Testament writings from which to translate; instead, they translated from Greek and Latin into various languages.

The first known English translations of Scripture were translated from the Vulgate—a Latin translation that used the most ancient Greek texts for translating the New Testament. A New Testament translation into Latin using Greek texts had been completed by 410 AD. By the 1380's, John Wycliffe had translated and was producing

Questions Regarding Baptism

hand-written copies of the English Bible, using the Latin translation primarily because that was his only access to Scripture. The history of the Bible—translated into the various languages of the world—is fascinating. And translations came about with great sacrifice, costing some theologians their lives for attempting to make the Bible accessible to all. The entire Bible has been translated into over six-hundred different languages. Multiple English translations have referenced various translations—both Greek and Latin—using the Greek name for Jesus instead of using the Hebrew version.

Next, let's consider why it's inappropriate for religious groups such as the *Sacred Name Movement* to insist that English Christians use the Hebrew name for the Savior. The Hebrew language, like most languages, has gone through various stages of change. The language spoken by the Hebrews entering the Promised Land, under the leadership of Joshua, was entirely different than the language spoken by the Hebrews returning from Babylonian captivity. The Hebrew language became influenced by seventy years of exile in Babylon, and it took on obvious changes. During this exilic period, the Hebrews adopted a language style called Aramaic. Mary and Joseph would have spoken this language, not Old Testament Hebrew.

Time and circumstances change all languages. Further, Galilee, the northern part of Israel where Jesus' parents raised him, had a different accent than their southern neighbors in Judea. Consider the dilemma translators must contend with. One article explains, "The Hebrew name of the historical Jesus is probably pronounced '*Yeshua*,' although this is uncertain and depends on the reconstruction of several ancient Hebrew dialects."[13] The Hebrew language experienced tremendous change throughout the approximately two thousand years from Abraham to Jesus. The same is true for the two thousand years after Christ. It is possible that if we called the Hebrew name of the Savior in baptism, we would pronounce it differently compared to how the angel, his parents, friends, and disciples would have spoken His name. So, the fact that the spoken languages went through significant transitions over time brings into question the argument of the *Sacred Name Movement*.

Finally, let's recap some of the issues with the *Yeshua* movement arguments and consider numerous Scriptures that offer direction for a valid New Testament baptism using the name of Jesus.

- We have a specific directive from preserved Scripture to call upon the name of Jesus for our needs, to combat satanic attacks, and for baptism. "And whatsoever ye do in word or deed, do all in the name of the Lord Jesus, giving thanks to God and the Father by him" (Colossians 3:17). This Scripture was first written in the Greek language, so it would have used the Greek name of the Savior, not the Hebrew. Our translation into English translated the Greek name, not the Hebrew; therefore, we are scripturally accurate when we baptize into the name of Jesus. To insist that we use *Yeshua* instead of Jesus is demanding something for which we have no known written source of New Testament Scripture. Our English translations of Scripture are transcribed and translated directly from the oldest known sources of Scripture: Greek and Latin, not Hebrew.

- The Bible, neither in the Old Testament or the New Testament, states a preference for a particular language; contrariwise, it used a variety of written languages, the first being Moses' language, of which scholars have few details. The written languages were primitive and still in emerging stages during this time. The Classical Hebrew, in its evolving and various dialects, became the common language of the Old Testament until the routing of Jerusalem by the Babylonians. Aramaic became the language of the Jewish people after the Babylonian captivity. Because of the diaspora of the Jewish people throughout the Roman Empire—its common language being Greek—scholars translated the Old Testament into Greek. The Septuagint is the most commonly-know, Greek translation of the Old Testament, and it translated the name of God into the Greek language; it did not retain the Hebrew rendering of God's name. And all ancient copies of the New Testament in the Greek language likewise used the Greek translation for God's name. They did not use God's name in the Hebrew form.

- There is an interesting event recorded in the New Testament Book of the Acts of the Apostles (Acts 2). At the birth of the church, when Christ's disciples waited in the upper room for the promised descent of the Spirit, they undoubtedly prayed in the standard Hebrew language, Aramaic. Suddenly, the Holy Spirit filled them, and a supernatural transformation of their common Hebrew language took place: these Hebrew followers of Christ worshiped God in a multitude of languages that they had not learned. Representations of each of these languages were present in Jerusalem for the Jewish Holy Day and witnessed this miraculous event. The phenomenon of Pentecost included various languages from every direction of the world, not just the Hebrew language. God is the God of all languages. And the Savior's name, translated into any language, is valid for baptism.

- Since Hebrew speaking scribes preserved the oldest known copies of the Old Testament, these are dominantly written in Classical Hebrew (also called Biblical Hebrew), but these transcriptions were not necessarily written in the exact language in which they were first spoken. We aren't sure what language Adam, Eve, and God spoke in the Garden of Eden. From Genesis chapter one to chapter eleven, the people spoke a common language: "And the whole earth was of one language, and of one speech" (Genesis 11:1). This singularly spoken language of the first chapters of Genesis was unique from the written language Moses used some twenty-five hundred years later to record the Genesis, oral history. As a curse from God for the sinful attitude at Babel, the common language of Genesis became confused among various family groups. God understood each of these various languages. Later, Abraham, the father of the Hebrew people, having moved from the Mesopotamian Valley into the land of the Canaanites, spoke a different language than Israel's beloved psalmist and king, David. We cannot be sure in what language God carved the Ten Commandments. The written script of Moses was a newly developing written language. The Classical or Biblical Hebrew "… comprises several evolving and overlapping dialects."[14] The post-exilic (after the Babylonian captivity of the Jewish people)

Old Testament books included the Aramaic language. In the third century BC, due to the many Hebrews throughout the Roman Empire who didn't speak their native language, scholars interpreted the Old Testament into various Greek translations. Scholars aren't in agreement as to what language God used on the palace wall of the Babylonian King Belshazzar (Daniel 5). Daniel was able to interpret the writing, but we aren't sure if he knew the language or if God gave him a supernatural interpretation—probably the latter. As for the New Testament, there are no known ancient copies written in the Hebrew language; instead, all known ancient texts are in the Greek language.

- Interestingly, some New Testament writers quoted from Greek sources of the Old Testament instead of the Classical Hebrew. Some Greek translations of the New Testament have Jesus quoting from the Septuagint, though this does not prove Jesus literally quoted from the Greek. The written languages are humanly established, not God invented. From this condensed discourse of the history of the spoken and written languages of Scripture, we conclude there was no preferred language God used: the languages evolved throughout the centuries, and God relied upon humanly established languages to record and preserve His Word. God's saving name, Jesus, is hallowed in hundreds of different dialects.

- An underlying—though perhaps unspoken—theme of the *Yeshua* proponents is that the name of the Savior used in Scripture should be addressed differently than all other names in the Scripture. Such names as Peter, James, and John are okay to have been converted into English. They contend, however, that the name *Yeshua* must not be translated. Some within this movement go so far as to suggest an apostate church changed the New Testament from its original Hebrew and used a Greek name for the Savior, associating the Greek translation of the name of Jesus with paganism, particularly the Greek god Zeus, the god of sky and thunder. The idea has no factual merit; instead, it gains momentum only among religious conspiracy movements mostly using the Internet to perpetuate intrigue and falsehood. The notion even exists that truth is being purposefully withheld from us, and when taken to an extreme, this notion is so inflexible that it suggests there is an original New Testament text written in Hebrew but purposefully hidden from us. However, there is absolutely no scholarly proof for this theory. Further, if we cannot trust the New Testament translations we have, the church is left in utter chaos, without direction, for we would have no Scripture to direct us. This would also suggest that God didn't make provision for us to have the truth, contrary to His Word that states, "Heaven and earth shall pass away, but my words shall not pass away" (Matthew 24:35).

- The *Yeshua* movement would not only affect English-speaking people, but it would also transcend all languages, and every language would have to use the Hebrew language when referencing the name of the Savior. This is isolationism in one specific area of Bible interpretation and is contrary to acceptable norms of Bible translation.

- Whether we say *Iēsoûs*, Jesus, *Yeshua*, *Yehoshua*, or the English equivalent for Jesus, Joshua, the Savior's name was a common name in the first century. It was not unique when the angel pronounced to Christ's parents that they should call their child *Yeshua*. The significance is in the meaning of the name: Jehovah Savior, or Jehovah has become salvation. That meaning remains in the transliteration: when we say Jesus, we are calling upon our Savior, the God of the Old Testament Incarnate in Christ. In the technicality ascribed by the *Yeshua* movement, we would have to be more specific when calling on the Savior's name, or else we may unknowingly pray to a false *Yeshua*. We would need to clarify the *Yeshua* to whom we are praying: the *Yeshua* born to Mary and Joseph; the *Yeshua* born during the time of the wise men; the *Yeshua* that was crucified by Pontius Pilate. This is insulting to God, as if He isn't omniscient and aware we are calling out specifically to Him when we call upon His saving name, Jesus.

- Whether we use the Hebrew *Yeshua*, the Greek *Iēsoûs*, the English Jesus, or the Spanish *Jesús*, we are addressing our Lord and Savior Jesus Christ—God Incarnate—through the use of various language translations and transliterations. All the power of His name in any language is available to accomplish any task at hand: salvation, peace, healing, deliverance. "And whatsoever ye shall ask in my name, that will I do, that the Father may be glorified in the Son. If ye shall ask any thing in my name, I will do it" (John 14:13-14).

Throughout the centuries, man created the languages, and these have evolved and changed over time. God knows and speaks all languages. In His omniscience, He knows the thoughts and intents of the heart. He speaks the English language as well as isolated languages that are rare dialects. The entire Bible has been translated into more than two hundred and fifty languages, with portions of

Scripture translated into more than thirteen hundred languages. Each time this is accomplished, the name of the Savior is translated into the particular language being used. Our English biblical reference to the Savior in its full context is Lord Jesus Christ, and He proclaimed, "... All power is given unto me in heaven and in earth" (Matthew 28:18).

Consider again some of the Scriptures regarding the authority associated with the name of Jesus Christ. It is imperative that we proclaim Jesus' name in prayer, praise, and baptism.

> Whatsoever ye shall ask the Father in my name, he will give it you.
>
> John 16:23

> Neither is there salvation in any other: for there is none other name under heaven given among men, whereby we must be saved.
>
> Acts 4:12

> That at the name of Jesus every knee should bow, of things in heaven, and things in earth, and things under the earth ... .
>
> Philippians 2:10

> And whatsoever ye do in word or deed, do all in the name of the Lord Jesus....
>
> Colossians 3:17

Questions Regarding Baptism

To be consistent, English speaking, Christian congregations should baptize converts using the anglicized name of the Savior—Jesus. This name is derived from the oldest known copies of Scripture and is sufficient to wash away one's sins.

Ananias of Scripture emphasized not only the authority of the name of Jesus, but he expressed the urgency of acting upon that authority when he proclaimed to Saul, "And now why tarriest thou? arise, and be baptized, and wash away thy sins, calling on the name of the Lord" (Acts 22:16).

As English-speaking Christians, it is proper to use the name of the Lord Jesus Christ at all occasions: baptisms, dedications, praying for the sick, casting out demons, and pronouncing blessings.

Speak the name reverently. Utter it with faith. Shout it in praise. Say it often in prayer. Pronounce it at every Christian baptism. Jesus!

Endnotes

1   International Masters Publishers AB, 2008, p 11

2   Yonatan Adler, *Watertight and Rock Sold*, (Biblical Archaeology Review, Spring 2021), pp. 44-51

3   Dr. William Smith's Dictionary of the Bible. Volume 1, Houghton, Mifflin, and Company, Boston, MA, The Riverside Press, 1894, p 238

4   Wuest's Word Studies from the New Testament, Volume 1, Kenneth S. Wuest, Wm. B. Eerdman's Publishing Company, Grand Rapids, MI, 1973

5   The Message (MSG) Copyright © 1993, 1994, 1995, 1996, 2000, 2001, 2002 by Eugene H. Peterson

6   An Encyclopedia of Religions, by Maurice A. Canney, London: George Routledge & Sons, ltd. New York : e. p. Button & Co. 1921 https://archive.org/stream/encyclopaediaofr00cann/encyclopaediaofr00cann_djvu.txt

7   Holy Bible, New International Version®, NIV® Copyright © 1973, 1978, 1984, 2011 by Biblica, Inc.® Used by permission. All rights reserved worldwide.

8   Francesco Arduini, *The Pandemic Orgin of Child Baptism,* (Biblical Archaeology Review, Spring 2021), pp. 70-71

9   Wikipedia, https://en.wikipedia.org/wiki/Lingua_franca

10   Wikipedia, https://en.wikipedia.org/wiki/Koine_Greek

11   The Messiah's Name: Jesus, Not Yahshua, Daniel L. Seagraves, Morris Publishing, Keamey, NE, Copyright 1996, p 16

12   Ibid.

13   Wikipedia, http://en.wikipedia.org/wiki/Yeshua_name

14   Ibid., http://en.wikipedia.org/wiki/Hebrew_language